A new look at Treasures
of Archaeology

For centuries people have been trying to find out more about ancient civilizations. Yet our picture of the past is constantly changing as archaeologists continue to make new discoveries about life long ago. Modern archaeology is a fascinating form of detective work which requires amateur and expert alike to painstakingly piece together the long-lost clues to life in earlier times.

This beautifully illustrated book describes some of the most famous archaeological finds and re-enacts what they tell us about people of the past. The information on each find is arranged in the order in which it happened in real life. First there is a dramatic reconstruction of everyday life or of an episode in history which has since been buried, in its own way, by time. Next there is an exciting account of the discovery of each site and the treasures it contained. Finally, a quiz or practical project explains more about archaeological techniques or shows you how to make your own model artefact.

Foreign words and archaeological terms (italicized) are explained in the text or in the illustrated glossary.

ARCO

Acknowledgements

Author: Michael Gibson

Adviser: Bruce Welsh, MA,
Institute of Archaeology, London

Managing Editor: Trisha Pike

Editor: Su Box

Art Editor: Adrian Gray

Picture Researcher: Julia Calloway

Projects Adviser: Krysia Brochocka

Illustrators:
Reconstruction artwork by Geoff
Hunt of Artists' Partners. Project
artwork by Tony Streek. Other
illustrations by Tom Stimpson,
except p. 63 by Eric Jewell.

Published by:

Marshall Cavendish Children's Books Limited,
58 Old Compton Street,
London W1V 5PA, England.

IN THE U.K., COMMONWEALTH AND REST OF
THE WORLD, EXCEPT THE UNITED STATES
OF AMERICA

Arco Publishing, Inc.,
219 Park Avenue South,
New York, N.Y. 10003, U.S.A.

IN THE UNITED STATES OF AMERICA

Library of Congress Cataloging
in Publication Data

Main entry under title: A New look at treasures of archaeology.
  Extent includes index.
  SUMMARY: Recreates eleven stories of the ancient world
and describes the diverse methods archaeologists used to piece
together these stories. Includes suggested projects relating to
each discovery.
  1. Archaeology – Juvenile literature.
2. Civilization, Ancient – Juvenile literature.
3. Treasure-trove – Juvenile literature.
  (1. Archaeology. 2. Civilization, Ancient.
3. Treasure-trove)
  1. Arco Publishing.
CC171.N48   930.1   80–11240
  ISBN 0-668-04958-8

ISBN 0 85685 829 3

Pictures

Air Photographs Collection of the
Norfolk Archaeological Unit/D. S.
Edwards 69B; Ashmolean Museum
69T; Stephen Benson 50; Courtesy
of the Trustees of the British
Museum 20, 24–26, 72B; China
Pictorial 54–55; Peter Clayton 19B,
31B; Rex Cowan 60; Crown
Copyright (NMR Air Photograph)
66B, 67; Michael Dixon 74; Horace
Dobbs 61B; Leslie Drennan 27, 32,
40, 45, 57; Fiore 37; French
Government Tourist Office 10–11;
Adrian Gray 13, 51; Michael
Holford 73; Courtesy of the Italian
State Tourist Office (E.N.I.T.) 36;
A. Keiller 66T; Manchester
University 19TL & TR; Mansell
Collection 18, 30BR; Marion
Morrison 48; Museum of London,
Department of Urban Archaeology
6–7; Radio Times Hulton Picture
Library 16, 30BL; D. N. Riley
67L; H. Roger Viollet 37TR;
Scottish Development Department
72T; Seaphot/Flip Schulke 60, 61;
Ronald Sheridan 17, 37L, 38, 49B;
Universitets Oldsaksamling 42–43.

Contents

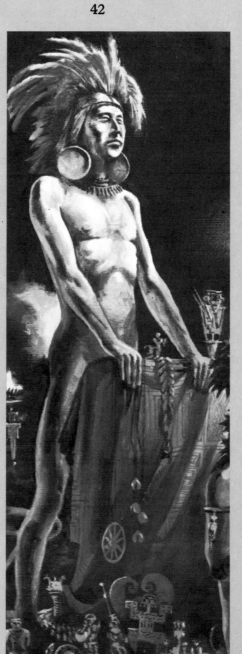

Puzzles of the Past

A huge giant of a man bellowed 'Put your backs into it'. Under the blazing Egyptian sun, Giovanni Belzoni, once an Italian circus strong man, glared at the sweating labourers before him. It was his task to find a way into the second *pyramid* at Giza. To the local Egyptians' astonishment and amusement Belzoni had searched long and hard for an entrance to the pyramid. They thought that everyone knew it was solid!

At last, on 28th February 1818, Belzoni found on one side of the pyramid a large block of granite which sloped downwards. He ordered his men to try to move it. Several days later the stone was shifted to reveal a pitch dark passageway leading into the pyramid. Most of it was blocked with large stones which the labourers cleared away to reveal a pivoted stone door. Gradually, the huge slab was levered up until a space wide enough for a man's body had been created.

In a fever of excitement, Belzoni crawled into the rock-cut tomb. A granite *sarcophagus*, or coffin, was sunk into the floor of the chamber. To Belzoni's deep disappointment, the lid was broken and the coffin was empty. The body of the *pharaoh* and the possessions which would have been buried with him had been stolen many years before.

At the time that Belzoni experienced his disappointment, *archaeology* was only beginning. This book traces its development from an activity little different from grave-robbing or treasure-seeking to a fully fledged science. In the 18th century, people's enthusiasm and greed had been fired by the rich discoveries at the Roman

Left: Archaeologists conduct a rescue excavation at Watling Court in the city of London before the builders move in. Many Roman remains have been found during the clearing of new building sites.

towns of Pompeii and Herculaneum in Italy, which had been buried beneath layers of lava and volcanic ash. Later, in the 19th century, the general public was excited by the successes of Heinrich Schliemann, who uncovered the remains of Troy in Turkey. Meanwhile, in the north of Europe, Scandinavians were unearthing a series of mysterious Viking burial ships.

As the years went by, genuine professional archaeologists appeared who took much greater care in their excavating. They studied each *occupation layer* and carefully recorded the exact position of every find. Nevertheless, archaeology remained intensely exciting. In the 1920s, Lord Carnarvon and Howard Carter discovered the pharaoh Tutankhamun's tomb buried beneath the rocks of the Valley of the Kings in Egypt. Meanwhile in Iraq Leonard Woolley was excavating the city of Ur, which lay beneath a mountain of earth.

It might seem that there could be nothing left to discover after these brilliant successes. But the truth is very different. In Colombia, South America, quantities of gold objects are still being recovered, and other glorious finds continue to be made all over the world. In China, the treasures of Shih Huang Ti, the first emperor of north and south China, are being unearthed at this very moment.

The 20th century has seen not only a revolution in archaeological techniques of discovery and dating, but also a new attitude to the past. Scholars all over the world are studying puzzling remains in order to discover as much as they can about the people who lived long ago. Faced with a mass of baffling fragments the modern archaeologist, like a detective, is engaged in the most exciting task of all, that of discovering the truth. By piecing together these scraps of evidence, he can reconstruct the ancient past.

The First Men

Silent men waited patiently behind the trees at the edge of the clearing. In the distance, they could hear shouting and the thunder of hooves as the frightened deer fled though the forest. Suddenly, the animals crashed into the man-made clearing and the men jumped out from behind their trees bellowing and waving their arms. The confused and terrified beasts dashed blindly through the clearing before dropping over the edge of a cliff and plunging some 40 metres on to the sharp rocks beneath. Waiting men rushed forward and stabbed the stricken deer with their fire-hardened wooden spears.

Once the hunt was over, the men set up camp for the night. They built a crude fence, to protect their families from prowling wild animals, and hastily erected shelters of branches and brushwood. Meanwhile, the women were busily engaged in cutting up the deer carcasses with their sharp flint knives. The men lit camp fires and soon great joints of meat were roasting over the flames.

When the hunters had satisfied their hunger and rested, they gathered together and marched in procession towards a small hole in the nearby cliffs. Each man lit the moss wick of a crudely hollowed-out stone lamp filled with animal fat and entered the dark forbidding tunnel that lay before him. After walking and crawling for some time, the men reached a great cave where the walls glistened with paintings of many animals: deer, antelope, bison and wild horses.

The men placed their lamps around the walls of the cave where the flames cast an eerie flickering light on the cave walls so that the paintings of the animals seemed to move. Then, with solemn faces, the assembled hunters began their strange worship ceremony. Slowly at first, and then with greater and greater speed, they danced around the chamber until each man was in a state of frenzy. Suddenly, a priest, dressed in a strange array of skins, leapt into the centre of the whirling, chanting dancers. Instantly, every man stopped and fell silent. The priest then proceeded to act out the day's hunt, until at last he sank exhausted to the floor.

When he had recovered, all but a few of the worshippers picked up their lamps and slipped silently out of the cave. The remaining men took crude bowls containing colours of various kinds and started to paint more pictures of animals on the walls. The artists depicted dying animals with spears sticking in their flanks. When they had finished, they bowed their heads and prayed that the spirits would send more animals to the area the following year, so that their families would remain well-fed and contented.

These events may well have been repeated many times in the long period known as the Old Stone Age. This period began about three million years ago and continued until about 10,000 B.C. The *nomadic* Old Stone Age people continually struggled for survival. As they travelled in search of food, the men fished, and tracked and killed the wild animals of the forest and plain. Meanwhile, the women collected roots and fruits, gathering whatever plants were in season.

For countless thousands of years, man had made little or no progress. His simple but efficient tools and weapons were made out of rocks such as flint, which could be easily split. However, man's greatest discovery was fire. With fire, he could warm himself in the coldest winter, and harden wooden tools to protect himself against the most dangerous of wild animals. Its light made it possible for him to penetrate into the deepest rocky caves and caverns. And it was here that the first painters developed their art.

Right: The end of the hunt. The terrified beasts plunge to their death as they try to escape from the hunters.

Four Boys and a Dog

Above: Cave paintings have been found in both northern Spain and central France.

In September 1940, during the Second World War, four young boys and their dog Robot went for a walk in the hills near Montignac in the Massif Central in France. While the dog rushed hither and thither through the trees, the boys chattered and laughed among themselves. After a time, they noticed that the dog had disappeared. Anxiously calling his name, the boys started to search through the undergrowth. Suddenly, they heard excited barking which seemed to be coming from among the roots of a fallen firtree. On pushing the roots aside, the boys discovered what appeared to be a deep hole. Not liking the look of it, they threw in a coin to see how deep the hole was. Almost immediately, they heard it ring against something solid.

Ravidat, the eldest boy, took out his knife and with the help of his friends hacked a way to the hole which he widened by removing some stones. As soon as it was large enough, Ravidat lowered himself down into the inky darkness and joined the excited Robot. For six or seven metres he wriggled like a snake through a narrow tunnel and then stopped to pull out his torch. As he reached forward to see how much further the tunnel went, he dislodged a stone, tripped over, and

10

found himself sliding down a steep slope. After tumbling down 20 or 30 metres, he hit the floor with a sickening thud.

Bruised and shaken but otherwise unhurt, Ravidat staggered to his feet. After some fumbling in the blackness, he found his torch. He switched it on and found that he was in a large cave. In a fever of excitement he called to the others and soon all four were standing in the cave.

As they looked around, the walls of the cave shimmered in the feeble torch-light. 'Look,' cried one of the boys, 'there are lots of lines on the wall over there.' Ravidat pointed his torch at the spot and the astonished boys found themselves staring at an enormous painting of an animal. Moving deeper into the cave, they came across more and more of these vivid pictures. By this time, the light from the torch had started to fade as the battery wore out, so that the boys were forced to turn back. When they reached the surface, they took a solemn oath to tell no one of their discovery and to come back the following day to explore the cave more fully. After carefully covering the entrance to the tunnel with branches, they made their way home as if nothing had happened.

Next morning, they carefully prepared for the expedition and set off on their adventure. They found

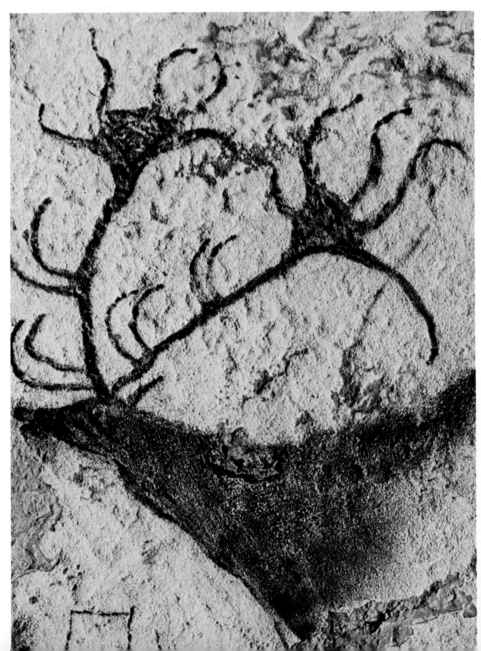

the entrance to the tunnel without difficulty and lowered themselves down to the cave. Soon, they had reached their previous discoveries. After a time, they came to a hole in the cave wall. On passing through it, they clambered down another 20 or 30 metres into a lower gallery.

With amazement they looked about them and saw the most extraordinary picture. It showed a man wearing an animal skin and a fantastic mask like a bird's head, lying before a dying bison whose mighty body was pierced by a spear. Painting after painting met their astonished gaze and the boys soon realized that they had made an important archaeological discovery.

During their history lessons, they had heard about similar cave paintings in Spain. Reluctantly, they decided that they could not keep such an important find secret.

The next day, they told their class teacher the whole story. He agreed to accompany them to the cave when school was over. Once in the cave, he realized that the boys had indeed made an important discovery. On returning to the town, he telegraphed the news to the Abbé Breuil, then the most famous archaeologist in France. A few days later, the Abbé confirmed the boys' belief that the paintings were prehistoric and the work of Old Stone Age men who had lived about 30,000 years ago.

When the Second World War was over, the Lascaux caves became a great attraction. By 1947, Ravidat and the other boys had become official guides to the site and they enlivened tourists' visits to the caves with their personal reminiscences. A proper entrance was constructed with air-tight doors and every effort was made to control the temperature of the caves. Unfortunately, in spite of all these precautions, the passage of hundreds of visitors each month brought about damaging changes in the temperature and humidity of the caves. It was only by limiting the number of visitors to the caves that the paintings were saved from fading completely.

Above: The caves contained only one picture of a man. He is lying helpless before an enormous wounded bison. The bird on the stake beside the man represents his soul.

Left: This painting shows a deer swimming with only its head and antlers above water.

Right: A section of the Lascaux cave wall covered with paintings of bison, wild horses and *aurochs*.

Prehistoric Paints

Prehistoric cave artists had to make paints before they could produce any pictures. Paint consists of two ingredients, known as the pigment and the medium. The pigment is the colouring material and the medium binds the pigment together, so that it does not turn to powder when the paint dries. Some modern paints are bound together with egg white or glue. Archaeologists think that prehistoric people may have mixed the pigment with blood, animal fat or beeswax.

The pigments used in prehistoric paints were fairly easy to obtain from minerals found in the earth. The painters were only able to mix shades of red, yellow and brown. The table below shows some pigments which prehistoric painters may have used and which are now available as refined chemicals.

Colour	Chemical pigment
Red	Anhydrous ferric oxide
Dark red	Anhydrous ferric oxide + carbon
Yellow	Hydrated ferric oxide
Dark yellow	Hydrated ferric oxide + a pinch of carbon
Dark brown	Hydrated ferric oxide + 10–15% carbon
Black	Carbon

The prehistoric painter mixed his paint in a hollowed-out stone or animal shoulder blade. He painted with his fingers, a brush (the sliced end of a stick or a few animal hairs) or a stamp (a twig covered with a pad of moss). Sometimes he crushed the pigment to produce powdered paint and blew it on to the rock through a bone or wood tube.

Usually the artist drew the outline of his picture in black or red and then filled in the space with colours. Sometimes the outline was scraped off the rock with a sharp flint tool when the painting was finished. The prehistoric painters were particularly good at making use of natural rock formations to give their pictures a three-dimensional effect.

Make some prehistoric paints

You will need: pigments (ask your chemistry teacher if you may experiment with the chemicals listed on the left), media (glue, egg white, honey, lard), several saucers, a stick, a paintbrush, some stones.

1. Mix the pigments to produce different colours. Too many pigments will make a muddy colour.

2. Combine the colours you like with a medium. You can experiment with different media to see which make the smoothest paint and to find out which stick best to the stones. Some stones will resist the paint and others will absorb it very easily.

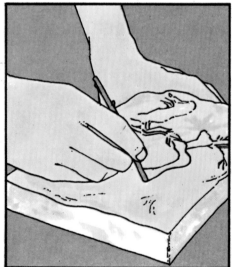

4. Mix light brown or sandy-coloured paint with plenty of water. Brush it across the surface of the plaster. Do not worry if it dries unevenly in the cracks as this will make it look like a real sandstone cave wall.

5. Use a very soft pencil or charcoal to draw the outline of an animal on your 'cave wall'. If any lines in the plaster remind you of a particular animal you can try to accentuate this. Look at the pictures of cave paintings in this section if you need some ideas.

Be a prehistoric painter

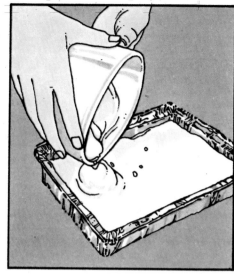

You will need: plaster of Paris, a tinfoil baking tray, water, a plastic bag, a bowl, a paintbrush, paints, newspaper.

1. As this may be messy, cover your working area with newspaper. Mix the plaster of Paris and water and pour into the baking tray.

2. When the plaster has almost set, press a plastic bag on the surface. Make dents and ridges in the plaster with your fingers. This produces an uneven, rock-like texture. Remove the bag after a few minutes and leave to set.

3. Carefully turn out the plaster when it has set hard. If you like you can scratch the surface to emphasize any cracks, hollows and ridges, so that it looks like a real cave wall.

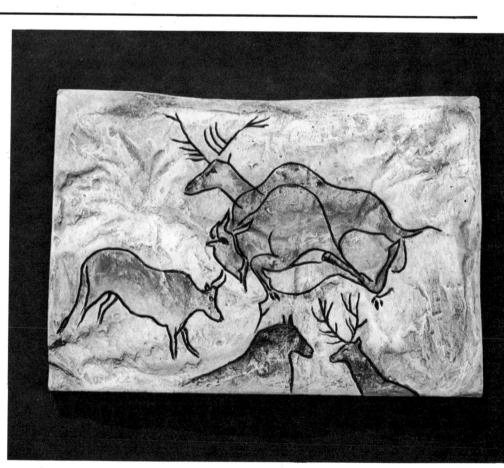

6. Fill in the outline of your picture with paints. You can use water colours or your 'prehistoric paints'. The painting will be more realistic if you choose the yellows, reds and browns which prehistoric men would have used.

7. Your completed project will look like a real cave painting.

The Child Pharaoh

Young Queen Ankhesenamun leant forward quickly and placed a small bunch of flowers on the shining gold mask that covered her dead husband's body. With the singing of the assembled priests filling her ears, the queen turned and walked slowly past the ranks of richly dressed nobles. Once outside the vast gloomy chamber, she stood for a moment blinking in the harsh light of the sun. It was over. Her husband, Tutankhamun, was dead and she must now attempt to cope with the ambitious priests and nobles on her own. Reluctantly, she admitted to herself that it was only a matter of time before she was forced to marry again. When her father, Akhenaten, had died in 1358 B.C., Ankhesenpaaten (or Ankhesenamun, as she was later called) had inherited the right to the throne and all the power that went with it. The man who married the queen would automatically become the pharaoh.

When Ankhesenamun and Tutankhamun ruled Egypt, in the 14th century B.C., it was one of the most powerful states in world history. The secret of ancient Egypt's wealth lay in the gleaming waters of the River Nile. Every year it flooded, covering the fields with a thin layer of rich reviving silt. As a result, a fertile strip of agricultural land ran through the yellow and brown of the desert. Year after year, bumper crops of wheat and barley grew in the fields to feed the teeming population of this long, narrow land.

In Egypt, the people thought that the pharaohs could act as go-betweens for the gods and ordinary people and that they were god-kings with unlimited power. In fact, this was far from the truth, for the priests had great influence as representatives of the Egyptian gods. There were many gods, the greatest of whom was Amun. Most Egyptians hoped that the king of the underworld, Osiris, would give them life after death. To the fury of the priests, Amenophis IV (1375–1358 B.C.) had dared to

overthrow the old gods and to replace them with the worship of only one god, Aten, who represented the disc of the sun. Renaming himself Åkhenaten, 'the servant of Aten', the pharaoh left the capital city of Thebes and built an entirely new capital at Tell el Amarna.

Unlike his predecessors, Akhenaten insisted upon living a simple family life. On his royal monuments, he and his wife were depicted as ordinary people, which hardly agreed with the traditional picture of a god-king who ruled Egypt from his golden throne on Earth before leaving this world to rule for eternity in the next.

On Akhenaten's death, the nine-year-old Tutankhaten was immediately married to his close relative Princess Ankhesenpaaten and became the pharaoh. Soon, the young couple were placed in an impossible position. Brought up to believe in Aten, they had to face growing pressure from the priests of the old gods to return to the old faith and the old capital. Tutankhaten was persuaded to return to Thebes when he was about 15 years old. Sadly, he ordered Akhenaten's beautiful capital, Tell el Amarna, to be totally destroyed. The old gods and their priests had triumphed. In acknowledgement of their victory, Tutankhaten changed his name to Tutankhamun.

His early death has given rise to a great deal of speculation. Perhaps Tutankhamun was murdered by the priests of Amun who feared that he would return to the worship of Aten as soon as he was powerful enough. Perhaps he had an accident or died suddenly of disease. The burial of the 18-year-old pharaoh seems to have been arranged with great haste. Did the priests have something to hide? It is unlikely that we shall ever know for sure.

Right: Queen Ankhesenamun takes a last look at her husband's coffin while the mourners wail and chant.

14

The Silent Valley

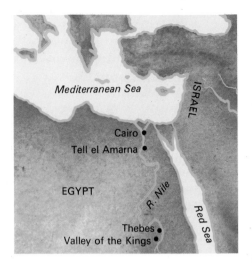

Above: The Valley of the Kings lies close to the ancient Egyptian capital of Thebes.

The Valley of the Kings is a gash in the Theban hills, separated by burning sands from the cooling waters of the Nile. In this desolate spot, up to 40 Egyptian pharaohs were buried more than 3000 years ago. It was here, in 1922, that one of the most spectacular archaeological discoveries of all time was made.

Generations of archaeologists had already patiently searched the valley, so that the experts predicted that nothing worth finding remained undiscovered. In spite of this, a keen amateur archaeologist called Lord Carnarvon decided to continue the search with the help of Howard Carter, a professional excavator. For several years, Carter carefully searched the valley without making any startling finds.

When their money began to run out, Carter decided to spend the last few precious months excavating a rock fall near the tomb of Rameses VI. After only nine days, Carter excitedly telegraphed his employer: 'At last have made wonderful discovery in the Valley a magnificent tomb with seals intact.' Carnarvon hurriedly returned to the *site*, and found that his workmen had uncovered a flight of steps leading to a door bearing the royal seals of the pharaoh Tutankhamun. When the door was pulled down and

16

the passage beyond it cleared of rubble, a second door was found.

The archaeologists' discovered that this door had been opened, and resealed at some time in the past. They had hoped that this was an unrobbed tomb, but the later seal showed that it had been opened and probably pillaged. The two archaeologists overcame their disappointment. No doubt a great deal could be learnt about this little-known pharaoh from what remained in the tomb.

Above: In the burial chamber, Carter found four golden shrines (inside each other). This picture shows him opening the last door to discover the immense sarcophagus within.

On 26th November, Carter bored a small hole in the door and peered through. For what seemed a long time, there was silence. Carnarvon could stand it no longer and asked, 'Can you see anything?' 'Yes,' replied Carter, 'Wonderful things.' Inside the antechamber lay gilded couches, a gold and silver throne, boxes of preserved food and hundreds of precious objects. From the disordered state of the treasures,

it seemed certain that thieves had been caught in the act of robbing the tomb, that a struggle had taken place and that the robbers had been bundled out of the area. The guards must have reblocked and resealed the door without waiting to clear up the mess.

Carter spent the next two months patiently photographing, recording and treating everything in the antechamber. He had already discovered the door to the burial chamber, but it was not until 17th February 1923 that the excited archaeologists broke through this door. They came face to face with a great golden box-shaped shrine. This turned out to contain four shrines, one inside the other. The last one held an enormous *sarcophagus*, or coffin, made out of yellow quartzite. Beneath the lid (which was so heavy that it had to be winched off), lay three more coffins in the shape of the pharaoh, one inside the other. The last coffin, made of gold and weighing about 135 kilograms, held the mummified body of Tutankhamun, dressed in the royal regalia. The head and shoulders of the dead pharaoh were covered by a magnificent golden death mask, and as the archaeologists looked down at this precious find it seemed to them that the face of Tutankhamun stared back at them. On his chest lay a tiny bunch of dried flowers.

For the first time in the world's history the entire tomb of an Egyptian pharaoh had been discovered. The find fired the imagination of people all over the world and tourists flocked to Cairo to visit the archaeological museum which contained the treasures.

Right: This golden death mask appears to be an exact likeness of Tutankhamun. It rested immediately on top of the pharoah's bandaged face and is life-size. The king is protected by a sacred vulture and cobra on his forehead.

Mummies

The ancient Egyptians (who were at the height of their power from about 3000 to 300 B.C.) believed that, if the dead were to enjoy their lives in the next world, their names had to live on for ever, their bodies had to be preserved and their corpses equipped with everything they would need. These conditions were fulfilled by providing the dead with documents containing their name and life history, by mummifying, or preserving, the corpse, and by providing it with food and drink and with helpers (in the form of statues and pictures).

The gruesome process of *mummification* was thus essential to enable the soul to continue life (re-united with the body) in the next world. Skilled experts first removed the dead person's brain by dragging it out through the nostrils with a special hook. Then, the chest was opened and the liver, lungs and intestines removed. These were carefully preserved and placed in storage jars known as *canopic jars*. However, the heart, which the Egyptians believed to be the source of intelligence, was left in the body. Then the whole corpse was covered

in a chemical called natron (a mixture of sodium carbonate and bicarbonate) and left to dry. Once the body tissues had dried out, which took about 70 days, the body

Below: Howard Carter removing the consecrating oils covering Tutankhamun's third and golden coffin. These oils had been poured over the coffin during the burial service and formed a thick sticky substance, which had to be peeled off by hand before the lid of the coffin could be raised.

cavity was washed out and packed tightly with linen and spices. This gave the corpse a life-like shape and appearance.

Now the body was ready for bandaging. First, each finger and toe was bound in fine linen strips; then each limb, and finally the whole body was swathed in bandages. Unfortunately, the ointments which were rubbed on the body before bandaging (supposedly to protect the corpse) actually brought about its decay, burning away its flesh and even attacking the bones. When Tutankhamun's body was examined, the archaeologists found that only his head, and hands and feet (which were covered with gold sheaths) had been perfectly preserved. Ironically, the bodies of poor Egyptian labourers who were unceremoniously buried in dry sand were perfectly preserved.

Many mummies disintegrate as soon as they are exposed to the air, thus making the long and expensive mummification process useless in the end. Nowadays mummies are often X-rayed. This is a good way of studying a mummy without unwrapping the bandages. Such X-rays can tell archaeologists a great deal about the state of the corpse and whether there are any interesting objects hidden among its bindings.

In order to protect the mummy, *amulets* or lucky charms of various kinds were placed on the body and between the bandages. There were, for instance, 143 precious objects tucked into Tutankhamun's wrappings. These included gold finger-stalls, sandals, gold rings, necklaces, bracelets, daggers and amulets. Perhaps the most important was the model of the *scarab* or sacred beetle. This was placed on the heart in order to carry a message asking the heart not to speak out against the spirit when it was being tried by the god Osiris, who judged all spirits wanting to live in the underworld.

Once the mummification process was over, the priest used water and incense to perform the ceremony of 'Opening the Mouth'. Egyptians believed that this enabled the dead person to become a *ba*, or living soul, with the strength to fight off the evil spirits which would attack it on its long journey to the underworld. On reaching the underworld, the ba made its way to the vast Hall of Judgement where the god Osiris sat in state. In the centre waited Maāt, the goddess of truth, who weighed the dead person's heart in a balance against the feather of truth. Thoth, the ibis-headed god, checked the scales and made a record of the result. If the two pans of the scale balanced exactly, Osiris cried, 'Let the soul of the dead go wherever he wishes and mingle with the gods and the spirits of the dead'. If the scales failed to balance, the heart was given to a frightful monster called Ammit or 'Devourer of the Dead'.

After judgement, however, the successful spirits were supposed to live in eternal happiness and untroubled luxury in Osiris's kingdom.

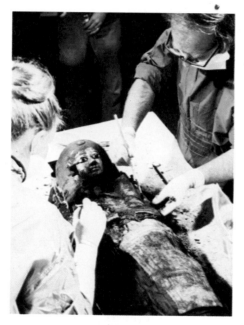 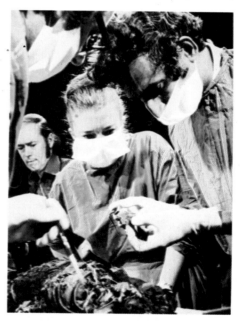

Above, both: Dr David and her team at Manchester University carefully examine a mummy.

Below: On 9th June 1886 an archaeologist called Maspero unwound the bandages covering the remarkably well-preserved mummy of Rameses II.

The Key to the Sacred Writings

Before the beginning of the 19th century, no one had succeeded in understanding *hieroglyphs*, the sacred writing with which the ancient Egyptians covered so much of their temples and monuments. Then, in 1799, what proved to be the key to the mystery, the Rosetta Stone, was discovered by a section of Napoleon Bonaparte's expeditionary force who were digging the foundations of a fort near Rosetta on the west bank of the River Nile close to the sea. The stone bore an inscription in praise of Ptolemy V Epiphanes, the king of Egypt in 196 B.C. The inscription was written in three different scripts: hieroglyphic, demotic (a kind of Egyptian shorthand) and ancient Greek.

In spite of this discovery, there was no immediate breakthrough and scholars remained as confused about the meaning of hieroglyphs as ever. However, Jean-François Champollion, a French schoolboy and a gifted linguist who could understand six different languages by the time he was 16, became fascinated by hieroglyphs. For many years Champollion studied them as a hobby. People had suggested that *cartouches*, or oval frames, surrounded the names of the pharaohs on the Rosetta Stone. Accepting this, he concentrated on the hieroglyphs and, after a time, he identified the cartouches of Cleopatra and of Ptolemy. By careful comparison, he was able to work out which hieroglyphs represented the letters *p*, *o* and *l*. It was obvious that the second, fourth and fifth signs in the hieroglyphic group meaning 'Cleopatra' coincided with the fourth, third and first signs of the equivalent group for 'Ptolemy'.

Champollion then hit on the idea that each of the hieroglyphic pictures or letters represented sounds. Thus, he had arrived at a partial solution to the problem. As a result of years of painstaking work, Champollion was able to

20

Above: The Rosetta Stone.

build up a list of 24 picture signs which represented the consonants of the modern alphabet. Although there were no vowels in early inscriptions, the consonant hieroglyphs were never used by themselves. They were always supplemented by *determinatives* or qualifying hieroglyphs which indicated the general meaning of a particular hieroglyphic group.

In September 1822, Champollion announced his success to an incredulous world. Many scholars refused at first to believe that he had discovered an answer to the problem which had baffled them for

generations. However, as the years went by, it became clear that Champollion's claims were justified and he was received with honour wherever he went. At the height of his fame, in the late 1820s, he made a triumphant visit to Egypt. During his stay he not only translated numerous hieroglyphic inscriptions but even turned his hand to a little practical archaeology. Unfortunately, Champollion was not to enjoy his success for very much longer as he died in 1832.

Right: The cartouches which aided hieroglyphic translation.

More about the alphabet

The hieroglyphs which the ancient Egyptians carved or painted on their temple walls were originally pictures of animals and everyday things. Gradually the pictures came to represent sounds rather than objects. A series of signs grouped together spelled out a word phonetically or by its sounds.

The English word 'famine', below, is spelled in hieroglyphs. The picture of the starving man at the end of the word is a determinative, or clue, to the meaning of the word. At first, the ancient Egyptians had no signs for vowel sounds such as *a*, *e*, *i*, *o* and *u* and determinatives prevented them from confusing similar words.

determinative

= famine

F   M   N

Use the hieroglyphic alphabet chart to help you work out this short word.
Remember that the determinative will give you a clue. (The answer is at the foot of the page.)

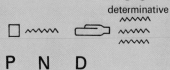

determinative

P   N   D

Now write a simple message in English and translate it into hieroglyphs using the alphabet chart on the right.

Egyptian mathematics

The ancient Egyptians were also expert mathematicians, which is why they were able to carry out the complicated calculations needed to design the pyramids.

They used signs to represent the numbers below 10, multiples of 10, 100 and 1000.

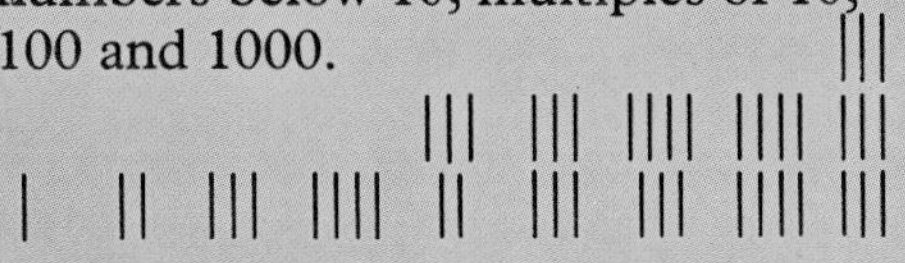

1	2	3	4	5	6	7	8	9

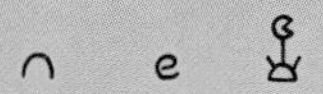

∩   e   𐦙
10 100 1000

Using these signs they could write down any number and, if necessary, carry out complicated arithmetic. The signs below represent what we would write as the number 1456.

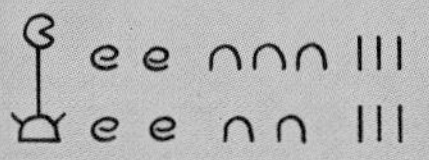

$$\text{(hieroglyphs)} = 1456$$

Can you work out what this number is? (The answer is at the foot of the page.)

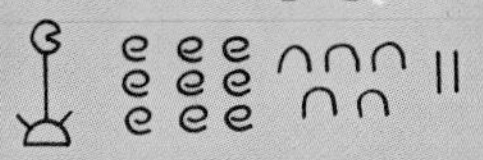

The Hieroglyphic Alphabet

Sign / Transcription	sound-value	= modern letter
vulture	glottal stop (as in bottle when mispronounced)	
flowering reed	I	i
two flowering reeds	Y	y
quail chick	W	w
foot	B	b
stool	P	p
horned viper	F	f
owl	M	m
water	N	n
mouth	R	r
reed shelter	H	h
folded cloth	S	s
pool	SH	s
hill	Q	k
basket with handle	K	k
jar stand	G (as in goat)	g
loaf	T	t
tethering rope	Tj	*t*
hand	D	d
snake	Dj	*d*
lion	L	l

P
O L Y S
T M

Ptolemy

K
I   O   P A T T
L   R A ?

Cleopatra

Answers

The hieroglyphic word spells 'pond'. The number is 1952.

The Temple City

The high priest of the temple stood on the top of the mighty *ziggurat* of Ur, looking down at the busy scene that spread out before him. Behind him, priests were singing the praises of the god and making their offerings to his statue. The high priest's keen eyes swept along the tiers of the great ziggurat with satisfaction. Its slightly curved walls covered with brightly coloured tiles reflected the burning light of the sun. It was truly a magnificent shrine.

Far below he could see great columns of people, clad in woollen robes and fleeces, crowding into the great open courtyards before the ziggurat to pray and make their offerings. Close by lay the giant silos storing baskets of grain, dates and figs grown on the temple estates or paid by the people as taxes. These were counted by careful clerks who recorded the amounts in *cuneiform* numbers upon clay tablets. It was the third millenium B.C., and Ur was a prosperous city.

Looking beyond the straight, crowded streets and the well-planned blocks of houses to the city's walls, he could see soldiers on guard at the mighty fortified gateways and the massive towers. None of their neighbours could hope to launch a surprise attack upon the city of Ur as long as the soldiers remained alert.

Outside the city walls, fields divided by irrigation canals, glinting in the bright sunlight, stretched away in the distance. Singing peasants moved slowly between the rows of crops, hoeing the rich black soil. The fields reached right down to the banks of the mighty River Euphrates, the source of life and death in this rich land of Mesopotamia. Even from this distance, the high priest could see the light playing upon its waters as it flowed sluggishly towards the sea. Fine ships made of bundles of papyrus reeds were hoisting their sails. The high priest almost envied the sailors who made their way to India and even beyond, returning with the luxuries which meant so much to the rich people of Ur.

As the high priest's eyes swept the city once more, he thought how curious it was that life was continuing as usual. Only a few days ago, the king had died and even now his successor was supervising his funeral. The high priest could imagine the scene, as he had witnessed several such ceremonies over the years.

Hidden from sight, workmen would have dug a deep shaft grave and lined its walls with the best bricks. Then the king's corpse, dressed in his finest robes and jewels, would have been placed on a beautiful *bier* in the tomb. Slowly, selected courtiers, soldiers and musicians would file into the tomb and group themselves around the body. Finally, a pair of asses would pull the dead king's chariot down a ramp into the grave. While the animals stood tossing their heads under the weight of the yoke, prayers and gifts would be offered to the gods. Each person in the tomb would take a tiny cup, drink its poisonous contents, and soon all would be lying on the ground in a drugged sleep. Quickly, soldiers would slip between the slumbering figures to kill the asses where they stood and silent workmen would swiftly shovel earth into the grave until it was full. Carefully, they would stamp down the soil and make way for the bricklayers who would seal the tomb for all eternity.

The musing high priest shivered at these morbid thoughts. Then, with a resigned shrug of his shoulders, he turned and walked over to his priests before the god's great shrine. He joined in their worship, thankful that the time for his death had not yet come.

Right: King Ur-Nammu built the ziggurat dedicated to the moon god Nannar, which dominated the great city of Ur.

'We have found the Flood'

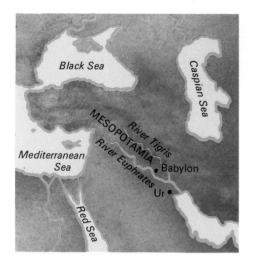

Above: Ur was on the banks of the River Euphrates which kept the farmland fertile.

Right: Sir Leonard Woolley (1880–1960), who was made famous by his excavation of the royal cemetery at Ur.

In 1922, a British archaeologist called Leonard Woolley began to excavate a great mound near the River Euphrates on the site of Ur, the home of the biblical father of the Jewish nation, Abraham. The *tell*, or mound, contained the remains of not just one city but of many which had been built on the same long-established site in Sumer (southern Mesopotamia).

About 5000 years ago the most common building material used in Mesopotamia (modern Iraq) was mud brick. To be strong, mud-brick walls had to be thick. As the Mesopotamians could not use mud bricks twice (and carting away the rubbish was expensive), the simplest thing to do when a wall collapsed was to level the surface of the ruins and build on top of them. As a result, the Mesopotamian cities rose higher and higher above the plain as the centuries passed.

When Leonard Woolley started to dig down through the tell at Ur, he found that there was a large number of different occupation levels (the city's remains from different periods in time) built one

Above: Arabs help to excavate the death pit at Ur.

on top of another. The earliest levels were at the bottom, the latest at the top. What Woolley did was to scrape away the surface of the ground until strips of dark earth appeared. These were the remains of the brick walls. Then he made trenches close to both sides of the wall and carefully brushed off any mud that was still sticking to the remains. In this way he was able to expose the ruins of the houses and

Below: The standard of Ur shows scenes from Sumerian life.

24

temples of ancient Ur.

At a depth of about 11 metres, Woolley reached a *stratum*, or layer, of decayed brick, broken pottery and rubbish. These finds alone would have made the excavation worthwhile, but even more exciting discoveries were made as Woolley unearthed some royal tombs. In one grave, that of Queen Shub-ad, he found gold cups and vases, and two vessels made of copper and silver. The queen, who was wearing a thick black wig adorned with a head-dress made of gold, lapis lazuli and carnelian, lay on a wooden bier surrounded by the skeletons of her ladies-in-waiting. At the end of one row of skeletons lay that of a harpist with his arm still lying across his instrument.

What did all this mean? Woolley decided that the position of the skeletons indicated that they had died peacefully. Presumably the ladies-in-waiting, soldiers and servants had chosen to die with their masters. Possibly they had taken poison or a drug to make them sleep before the workmen shovelled earth on top of them and sealed the tomb with bricks. Woolley estimated that these burials dated from about 2500 B.C. when the city of Ur was at the height of its power.

Right: This golden ram was found in the death pit at Ur.

After this magnificent discovery, Woolley dug still deeper into the tell. At a depth of about 12 metres, he came upon a layer of mud nearly three metres thick. Woolley realized that only a tremendous flood could have laid down such a thick band of *alluvium*. The land of Sumer must have been completely covered in water at some time. Woolley had read the histories of the kings of Ur describing how 'the flood came and after the flood kingship was sent down from on high'. Could this have been the great flood mentioned in the Bible and in the great Sumerian poem, the *Epic of Gilgamesh*? In 1929, after carefully considering all the evidence, Woolley sent off his famous telegram announcing 'We have found the Flood'.

Later archaeologists confirmed the fact that all the great towns of Sumer experienced the same disaster in about 4000 B.C. Here we see a great archaeologist arriving at a conclusion after considering both the archaeological and the written evidence. However, this does not prove conclusively that the events mentioned in the Bible and the *Epic of Gilgamesh* actually took place.

Woolley's discoveries also involved some developments in the art of restoration. Nearly all the beautiful objects he found had been crushed beneath a great weight of earth. Woolley stuck together the fragments he found with paraffin wax while they still lay in the ground. Once the mixture had cooled, each object was removed in one piece for further treatment. Later, the wax was gently warmed until it melted leaving a jigsaw of broken pieces. Then the jewellery and furniture was cleaned and restored to its original shape. Often, wooden frameworks had completely decayed and had to be replaced by modern reconstructions based on the fragments which had survived and on photographs taken of the object as it lay undisturbed and embedded in the earth.

25

Make a Sumerian Head-dress

Some of the most spectacular discoveries made by Leonard Woolley when he opened the royal tombs of Ur were in the grave of Queen Shub-ad. Surrounded by the skeletons of her ladies-in-waiting in their court finery, the queen was wearing a cloak of gold, silver and precious stones. The queen and each lady-in-waiting also wore necklaces, earrings and an ornate head-dress of gold and lapis lazuli. Unfortunately the skeletons and jewellery were crushed flat by the weight of the earth in the mound above the grave. However, with great patience, skilled and careful archaeologists were able to reconstruct most of Woolley's finds, restoring works of art (such as the head-dresses) to their former beauty and glory.

Above: A reconstucted Sumerian head-dress.

26

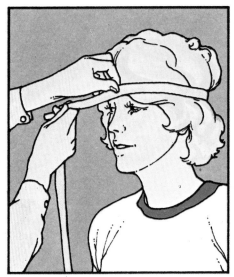

You will need: manilla card, a tape measure, a pencil, a ruler, rough paper, scissors, foil, a small stapler.

1. Measure the circumference of your head. Cut out this length plus 2 cm from a piece of manilla card, 3 cm deep.

2. Cover the card with two or three layers of silver foil. Gently rub the foil to smooth out any creases. Staple both ends of the card together so that it fits round your head just above your ears. Make sure that the ends of the staples are on the outside, so that there is no chance of scratching your head.

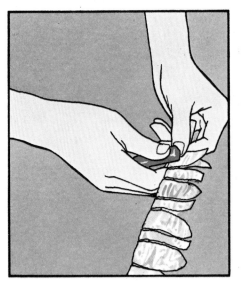

6. Cut out a strip of card, 1 cm wide, to the same length as the card in step **1**. Cover with two or three layers of foil. Hang the decorations from the strip of card and staple them in place. When the band is completely covered, staple it to the main head-dress.

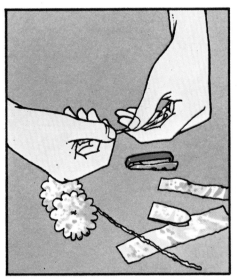

7. Cut out several narrow strips of foil. Fold over several times, and twist and squeeze the strips to make strong stems for the flowers. Using the template as a guide, cut out three flowers using a double thickness of foil. Make a hole in the centre of each foil flower.

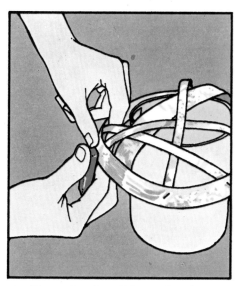

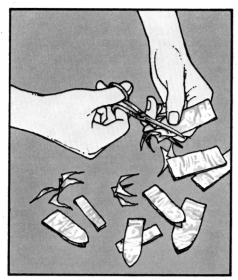

3. Measure across the top of your head (from ear to ear). Cut out a piece of manilla card, 3 cm deep, to this length. Cover this strip of card with two or three layers of foil and carefully staple each end of the card to form a cross-bar at the top of the head-dress.

4. To make the ribbons for the top of the head-dress measure across different parts of your head and cut strips of card (1 cm wide) to the right lengths. Cover the strips in foil. Staple the strips to either side of the main head-dress. You must now support your head-dress on a card cylinder.

5. Draw the designs for all the decorations on the paper. Cut out each design to make a template. Fold pieces of foil in half. Cut round the templates for the hanging decorations, making sure that there is a fold at the top of each motif.

8. Push one end of the stem through the hole, make a twist in the stem to keep the flower in place. Carefully wind the rest of the stem round the cross bar of the head-dress, until it is secure.

9. Carefully add the other flowers to the cross-bar to complete your head-dress.

The Greeks and Trojans

Over 3000 years ago, it is said, a bloody war took place between the ancient Greeks and the Trojans who lived in the north-west of modern Turkey. According to the Greek poet Homer, Paris, the handsome son of King Priam of Troy, fell in love with Helen, the lovely wife of King Menelaus of Sparta (a Greek city), and carried her off to Troy. Beside himself with rage, Menelaus went to his brother Agamemnon, the overlord of all Greece, and asked for his help. At once, Agamemnon declared war on Priam and by 1250 B.C. the Trojan War had begun.

King Agamemnon summoned all the Greek kings and their armies to him. They assembled a great fleet of ships and sailed to Troy, where they landed and laid siege to the magnificent city. For nine years the Greeks and Trojans fought beneath the walls of Troy without either side making any real progress. At last, Paris offered to settle the war one way or the other by meeting Menelaus in single combat. Menelaus eagerly agreed and the warriors met each other in front of their assembled armies.

Full of hatred Menelaus hurled his spear at Paris with such force that it pierced his shield and body armour. Before Paris had recovered, Menelaus hurled himself forward and smashed his sword down on the Trojan's helmet. Both the sword and the helmet were shattered by the violence of the blow. Throwing his broken sword aside, Menelaus seized Paris by the throat and started to strangle him with his helmet straps. Just as it seemed that the Greek king was the victor, the straps broke and Paris staggered away. Although the triumphant Menelaus hurled his spear at the retreating figure, Paris managed to escape.

The Trojan War continued as the years passed, and many Greek warriors became famous for their brave deeds. The greatest of all was the mighty Achilles. Once, to avenge the death of a friend called Patroclus (killed by Hector, King Priam's warrior son), he furiously attacked the Trojans and started to drive them from the battlefield. To his joy, he came across Hector and chased him three times around the city walls before stabbing him.

Not long afterwards, Achilles himself was killed. He was shot in the heel by Paris. However, Paris's days were also numbered and he died after being wounded by a poisoned arrow. Even this tragedy did not end the fighting. The Trojans still refused to return the beautiful Helen to her husband.

For a time it seemed that the Trojan War would go on for ever. Then Odysseus, the Greek king of Ithaca, thought of a cunning plan. He ordered the construction of a huge hollow wooden horse. When it was completed a number of Greek soldiers entered the horse through a cleverly concealed trapdoor and hid in its belly. The Greeks then broke camp and sailed away leaving the horse standing by the walls of Troy.

The Trojans began celebrating their victory with much rejoicing. At first they did not know what to do with the horse. But after a great deal of argument they hauled it into Troy. During the night, the Greeks, who had been waiting just out of sight of Troy, returned and silently made their way to the walls. The soldiers in the horse crept out of the trapdoor, killed the sentries and threw open the city gates. Within seconds, hundreds of shouting Greek warriors were rushing through the sleeping city and slaughtering their enemies without mercy. After looting the beautiful city they set it on fire and it soon burnt to the ground. At last, Helen was rescued by Menelaus and returned with him to Sparta where they lived in happiness.

Right: On entering Troy the Greeks showed the Trojans no mercy. In their fury they burnt the city to the ground.

Archæologist or Treasure-seeker?

Above: Schliemann excavated Hissarlik (the site of Troy) in Turkey and Mycenae in Greece.

The story of the Trojan War, recounted by the Greek poet Homer in the *Iliad*, has fired the imagination of countless people down the ages. A 19th-century German boy called Heinrich Schliemann was so excited by it that he swore that when he grew up he would seek out the site of ancient Troy. However, as he was poor, Schliemann had to forget this dream for many years.

He managed to get a job as a clerk with a firm of Dutch merchants and, during the 1840s, he taught himself to read and write seven languages. Later, he was sent to St Petersburg, then the capital of Russia, as his company's representative. This was the turning point of Schliemann's life, as he was extremely successful and became a very rich man. Despite his success, it was not until 1871 that Schliemann finally retired from business and devoted himself to seeking Troy and its treasure.

He started his first *dig* at a *site* called Hissarlik (in Turkey) overlooking the Dardanelles, the strip of water that divides Europe from Turkey. He was convinced that this was where Homer's heroes had fought and died. What made Schliemann so sure of this in the face of the disbelief of most of the

30

Above: A contemporary drawing of Schliemann's excavations at Hissarlik. It shows the deep pits he and his men dug in their unsuccessful search for Homer's Troy.

Below: Schliemann called these objects (discovered at Hissarlik) 'the Treasure of Priam'. Archaeologists have since proved that they date from before the Trojan War, when Priam ruled Troy.

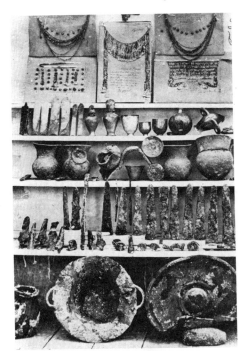

Right: This gold mask was found by Schliemann in a grave at Mycenae. He mistakenly believed it was the mask of Agamemnon, who was made famous in Homer's writings.

Below: Schliemann's second wife was chosen as the most charming of several girls suggested by the archbishop of Greece. Here, she is wearing some of the jewellery discovered at Hissarlik.

leading experts of his day? The simple answer is that he thought Hissarlik closely resembled Homer's description of Troy in the *Iliad*. While many historians dismissed this as a work of fiction, Schliemann accepted it as fact.

At the head of an army of workmen, he cut a great trench into the north face of the hillside. What he found was both bewildering and disappointing, for Schliemann identified more than seven occupation layers. Which was the Troy of Helen, Paris and King Priam? After two years' hard work he discovered some enormous stone walls at least six metres high.

These, he felt sure, must have been the ramparts of Troy.

To Schliemann's bitter disappointment, in spite of all his efforts, he discovered nothing truly exciting. Then, on 14th June 1873, the day before he was due to give up excavating the site, he found a gold object. Fearful of the effect that this find might have on his poverty-stricken workmen, he sent them away. Later, he and his wife, Sophia, secretly unearthed the treasure. The huge hoard contained nearly 9000 gold objects including necklaces, rings, buttons and a beautiful diadem. The excited archaeologist gave his wife the ancient jewellery to wear, exclaiming, 'Darling, this is the most beautiful moment of our lives; you are wearing the treasure of Helen of Troy!'

Schliemann was in fact incorrect, as he was later forced to admit. Helen of Troy had never worn this treasure. Later archaeologists proved that Troy II, as they called the layer where the treasure was found, dated from about 2300 B.C., whereas the Trojan War had taken place in about 1250 B.C.

Although Schliemann carefully searched the area where he had made his great discovery for three days, he did not find any more treasure. When he left Hissarlik the mound looked like a battlefield, criss-crossed by trenches. But now Schliemann was a famous man and could afford to ignore criticisms of his techniques. Determined that the whole world should recognize his success, he smuggled 'Priam's Treasure' out of Turkey and placed it on exhibition throughout Europe.

Although Heinrich Schliemann was not a great archaeologist in the technical sense, he made a great contribution to the world of archaeology by demonstrating the importance of classical literature as a record of history. For Schliemann, treasure was to be found in books as well as in the earth.

Make a Greek Helmet

In Homer's *Odyssey* and *Iliad* the heroes are mainly nobles such as Agamemnon and Menelaus. However, the footsoldiers played just as important a role in the fighting at Troy. As young men they would have had a good military training for at least two years (as was customary in most Greek city-states at that time).

Each footsoldier wore heavy armour. His body was protected by a breast plate and his legs with bronze guards called greaves. He was armed with a large round bronze shield and carried a long spear and a strong iron sword for hand-to-hand fighting. On his head each soldier wore a plumed helmet which had a protective nose piece and, sometimes, protective curved cheek pieces.

Above: This drawing shows a Greek footsoldier or *hoplite* with his armour and weapons.

You will need: a large round balloon, petroleum jelly, a bowl, a felt-tipped pen, newspaper, wallpaper paste, stiff paper, thick red paper, gold paint, scissors, glue.

1. Blow up the balloon until it is the same size as your head.

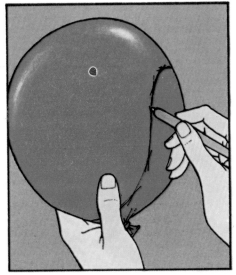

2. Use the felt-tipped pen to draw a rough outline of the helmet on the balloon. This will be your guide when you start to build up the papier mâché base. Smear petroleum jelly over the part of the balloon which is inside the line you have just drawn.

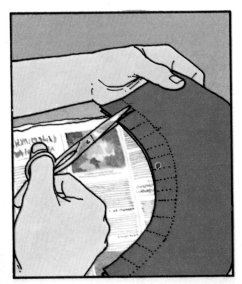

6. Cut two pieces of thick red paper to the shape of the crest, large enough to fit across the top of the helmet. Make cuts about 2 cm long along the inside (shorter) edge of the crest. Press out these tabs to the right on one piece of paper and to the left on the other.

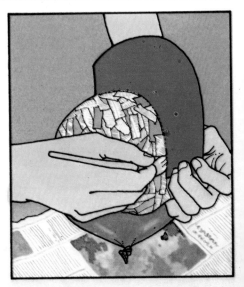

7. Glue together the pieces of paper except for the tabs. Leave to dry. Glue the tabs and stick the crest in place down the centre of the helmet. To make the crest really secure it is best to paste another layer of papier mâché over the tabs. Leave to dry.

32

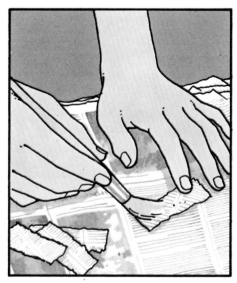

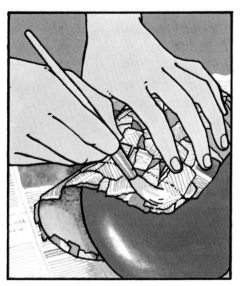

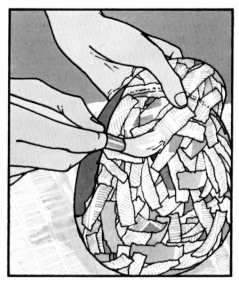

3. Tear the newspaper into small pieces. Mix the wallpaper paste in the bowl. Paste strips of torn newspaper on each side and stick them to the balloon. Leave to dry, then paste on another layer.

4. Cut a rectangular piece of stiff paper about 12 cm × 5 cm. Make short cuts every 2 cm along one side and stick the paper to the edge of the papier mâché – at the back of the helmet. The cuts in the paper will help you to ease the paper into place.

5. Continue to build up layers of papier mâché all over the helmet, using the stiff paper to support the curving neck piece. When you have added about 4 layers of papier mâché, leave the helmet to dry.

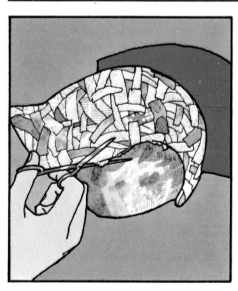

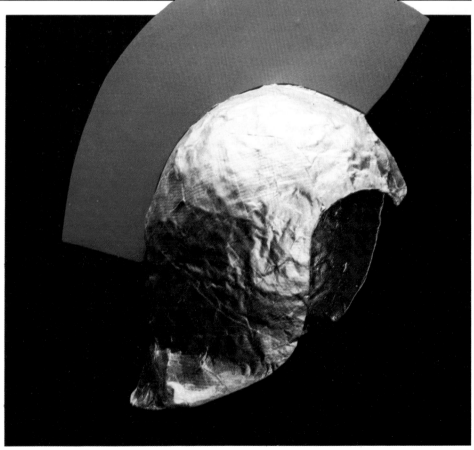

8. Burst the balloon. Trim away any rough edges on the helmet.

9. Carefully, paint the papier mâché with gold paint, taking care not to paint the crest, and your helmet is complete.

Death in the Morning

On the morning of 24th August A.D. 79, the Roman towns of Pompeii and Herculaneum were bathed in hot sunshine. People strolled along the straight, busy streets or stopped at one of the numerous stalls to buy refreshing wine or ripe fruit. Workers and slaves bought new-baked bread from one of the many bakeries while idlers wandered aimlessly through the streets staring at the notes and advertisements scrawled over many of the bare walls. Here and there dogs shook themselves, yawned, found a new spot and lay down in the shade.

The centre of Pompeii, the *forum*, was teeming with people. Criminal cases were being heard in the *basilica*, the town hall and law court of the town. The sound of laughter and raised voices was coming from the junior magistrates' offices. Merchants were gossiping at the cloth traders' hall. A few faithful citizens were making offerings to the gods in the lavishly decorated temples. In the markets, people haggled over the price of plump fruit, fresh vegetables and newly butchered meat.

As yet there were few people in the huge exercise ground, the *palaestra*, near the *amphitheatre* where there was to be a gladiatorial contest later that day. Nearby, some competitors sat in the shade testing and polishing their weapons. On the southern borders of the town, labourers were cleaning out the tiered seats of the theatre as yawning actors arrived to prepare for the day's work.

At the *thermae*, or baths, slaves were scrubbing the floors until the bright *mosaics* shone. They had stoked the ovens to heat the baths of steam and hot water, and put out pots of oil in the massage rooms, ready for the first customers.

All over the towns of Pompeii and Herculaneum, sweating slaves cleaned and polished, washed and scrubbed, and prepared food in finely furnished town houses where

sparkling fountains played in the antechambers. The mistresses of these luxurious homes gave their orders to their servants from the cool of little gardens behind their houses. Beds were made in the *cubicula*, or bedrooms, and the lamps in the dining room were filled with oil, ready for dinner, the main meal of the day.

Suddenly, the quiet was broken by an enormous explosion. The ground shook and the sun was hidden behind dense black clouds of smoke, cinders and flying rocks. The terrified citizens saw that the top of nearby Mount Vesuvius had completely disappeared. Flames and debris shot out of a gaping hole where the summit had been.

Many inhabitants panicked. Those living near the city walls and gates grabbed their most precious possessions and made good their escape. Others, who lived near the centre of the towns, were confused by the screaming and rushing crowds, and took refuge indoors.

Before long, dense clouds of sulphur gas had covered both the towns. Coughing and choking humans and animals alike collapsed, dying of suffocation. Mothers pulled their babies closer to them and little children buried their faces in their mothers' skirts. Dogs crept into corners or under furniture in a desperate effort to escape from the foul fumes. Even the people who thought they were safe indoors could not keep out the poisonous gas, and several families died in their own homes. Soon, there was silence except for the sound of the falling rain of ashes.

Pompeii was buried beneath a vast sheet of white ashes and volcanic stone, while the busy port of Herculaneum was covered by a layer of lava, or volcanic mud, 15 metres thick in places.

Right: During the disastrous eruption of Vesuvius many of the inhabitants of Pompeii died while fleeing in terror.

Cities from the Ashes

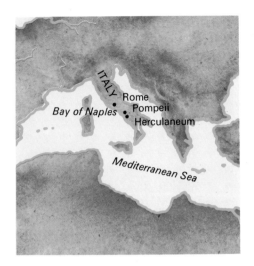

Above: The buried towns of Pompeii and Herculaneum are close to the Bay of Naples.

Below: An aerial view of the archaeological excavations at Pompeii shows that much work is still to be done.

As the famous excavator Sir Leonard Woolley pointed out in 1936, one of the best things that could happen to a city from an archaeologist's point of view was for it to be overwhelmed by a volcanic eruption. His reasons for making this curious statement were that the owners of the houses and shops in the disaster area had no time to rescue their belongings and robbers did not get the opportunity to steal anything of importance.

Thanks to the eruption of Vesuvius in A.D. 79, most of the buildings in Pompeii and Herculaneum were marvellously preserved. Apart from the roofs, houses and shops were often left standing. Much of the furniture and many household objects were protected by a layer of lava and ashes. In some rooms, petrified food was found on the tables just as the diners had left it when they fled for their lives. Perishable materials such as wood were *carbonized* and saved for modern eyes to admire. By a queer trick of fate, the disaster that struck the inhabitants of Pompeii and Herculaneum nearly 2000 years ago provided us with a clear picture of what life was like in prosperous provincial Italian towns during the first century A.D.

The first successful excavation at Pompeii took place under the direction of Rocco Gioacchino de Alcubierre, an engineer in the service of King Charles III of Spain and Naples. On 6th April 1748 the workmen uncovered a beautiful painted wall. From that moment the excavations at Pompeii have continued almost without pause and now more than half of the city can be visited.

Work on Herculaneum started

somewhat earlier, and so far about half the town has been uncovered. Unfortunately, the other half lies beneath the modern town of Erculano. As a result, the roofs of the present excavations have to be propped up with strong metal girders to avoid subsidence.

Some of the earliest finds were so badly damaged that the excavating archaeologists had to have them extensively repaired. This led to further developments in modern techniques of restoration. Unfortunately, at first, restorers were often easily discouraged and destroyed many valuable finds which they considered to be irreparable. Others mistakenly remodelled certain broken *artefacts* until they bore no resemblance to the original objects.

One of the most remarkable advances in the art of restoration was made by a friar called Antonio Piaggio. In 1753 a great collection of charred *papyrus* papers was discovered and, at first, the experts thought that it would be impossible to read them. However, Piaggio invented a machine rather like a complicated mangle which gradually unwound the papyrus rolls without causing much further damage. They were then separated from each other and reinforced with strips of linen so that the least charred pages could be read.

During the excavations, the archaeologists found a large number of carbonized objects. These were usually articles of furniture, sliding doors, screens, balconies and beams which had been burnt in the raging inferno that had engulfed the towns following the eruption. Fortunately, the atmosphere in which they were burnt was so short of oxygen that they were turned into charcoal instead of being reduced to ashes. In spite of the timbers' blackened and shrunken appearance, it is easy to recognize what the objects were. Ironically, if they had been buried in the soil, they would have rotted away. The only way that vegetable matter can be preserved successfully for centuries is through carbonization.

At Herculaneum, a great wave of boiling lava surged over the town. When the lava cooled down, it formed an airtight mass of solid rock. This blanket of lava preserved even the most perishable objects, fabrics and fragile furniture. Thus, by chance, the way in which Pompeii and Herculaneum were overwhelmed helped to preserve rather than to destroy the wealth of objects in the two towns.

Above: Part of the well-preserved wall painting at the Villa of Mysteries in Pompeii.

Above right: The Obillius family was overcome by the volcano's sulphurous fumes.

Right: The bodies of many of Vesuvius' victims were mummified in the lava.

Evidence from the Hollows

At the height of the Pompeii disaster in A.D. 79 about 2000 citizens were overcome by sulphur fumes. Ash from the volcano collected around their bodies, as they lay in their homes or in the streets, forming a hard outer shell. When the bodies rotted away, all that remained were hollow casts embedded in a thick protective layer of ashes.

When archaeologists first came across these hollows in the ash deposits, they were mystified. However, it was not long before they realized that they were natural casts rather than man-made holes. The archaeologists injected the hollows with wet plaster and, when the plaster had set, carefully chipped away the hard outer shell of ash. These plaster casts brought home the full horror of the catastrophe at Pompeii. The contorted features of these long-dead people make it easy to imagine what it must have been like on that last dreadful day.

1. Plaster is poured into a hole in the ash.

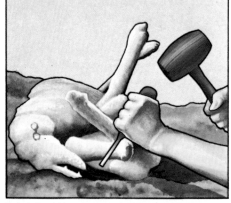

2. Ash is chipped away to show a plaster cast of natural remains.

Around the *palaestra*, or training ground, alone, the archaeologists discovered at least 100 bodies. Occasionally, it has been possible to work out what these people did for a living by studying the goods, such as tools and containers, which they had with them.

The plaster-cast method of reconstruction also helped the archaeologists to discover what kind of trees had lined the *palaestra*. Although the trees themselves had completely disintegrated, the spaces previously occupied by their roots still remained. These holes were filled with plaster and the casts examined by botanists, who, from the shape of the casts, were able to identify that the holes had been made by the roots of plane trees. Moreover, from the size and length of the roots, they were able to calculate the probable height and shape of the trees. Thus even 'invisible' evidence can give archaeologists clues to past history.

Left: The cast of a dog trapped in the house of Vesonius Primus records its death throes.

Below: A mosaic from Pompeii warns, 'Cave Canem' ('Beware of the dog'). This was no idle warning as many Roman families kept fierce guard dogs.

Make a Mosaic

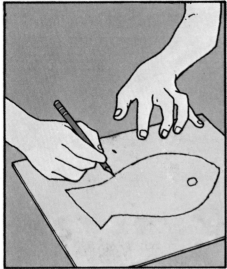

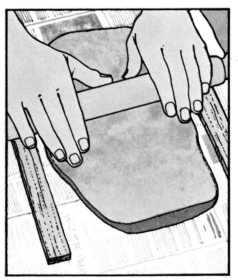

You will need: clay; newspaper, a rolling pin, two rulers, a knife, a pencil, scissors, glue, stiff cardboard, poster paint, a brush, paper.

1. Work out the design of your mosaic on the paper and copy the picture onto the stiff cardboard. It is best to keep to a few colours.

2. Cover your work surface with sheets of newspaper as this may be rather messy. Roll out the slab of clay with a rolling pin placed across two rulers. This will make sure the clay is of even thickness.

3. Cut the clay into narrow strips. Work out about how many strips will be needed for each colour of the mosaic. Paint the strips with the colours you have chosen for your design and leave the paint to dry.

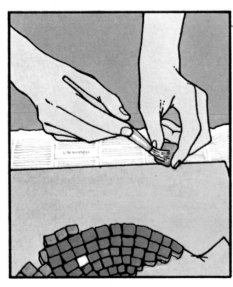

4. Cut the mosaic pieces needed for your design. It does not matter if they are not identical in shape and size. Glue small areas of the cardboard and stick the mosaic pieces in place. Leave the mosaic in a safe place to dry.

5. You can complete your mosaic by making a neat card border.

The Fury of the Norsemen

As the pale morning sun rose, dragon-headed longships with great square sails ploughed through the high seas off England until they reached an unprotected river mouth. Lowering their sails, they rowed silently up the gleaming waters until they came to a sleeping village. Silently the 'sea-wolves' (for so the Viking raiders were called) made their way to its gates and burst in on the unsuspecting inhabitants. After cutting down anyone who offered the least resistance, they made good their escape weighed down with booty and prisoners. Long before the local people could assemble an army, the Vikings had put their boats out to sea once more.

In the late 8th and 9th centuries A.D., the Viking people of Norway, Sweden and Denmark became the greatest warriors, traders and explorers of their time in Europe. The Swedes sailed down Russian rivers to the Black and Caspian Seas and made their way to Constantinople (modern Istanbul) and Baghdad, where they traded with rich Byzantine and Arab merchants. Norwegian explorers sailed to the Faroe Islands, Iceland, Greenland and finally America. The Danes, however, concentrated most of their energies on raiding the coastlines of western Europe.

The early Viking expeditions were led by fierce warrior chiefs who were famous for their strength, their skill with weapons and their luck in battle. Dressed in helmets, woollen tunics, trousers, and tall leather boots, they were as much at home on the pitching decks of their dragon-headed longships as they were on their small home farms.

When they were not raiding, the Vikings cultivated small fields of rye, barley and oats while their wives made butter and cheese from the milk of their herds. They lived in dark longhouses of between 12 and 30 metres in length. Inside, they slept on raised platforms that ran the length of the building.

There was little furniture except for the high chairs of the chieftain and his lady. Everybody else sat on benches or squatted on the floor. The Vikings warmed themselves and cooked their food over large fires in the centre of the room.

It was only fitting that each great warrior chieftain should be buried with great pomp in a fine ship (instead of a coffin) with everything he would need for the next life. The chief was laid out on a bier beside his ornate weapons and armour. Animals were slaughtered to provide him with food for his journey to *Valhalla*, the palace where the souls of the dead heroes were supposed to feast. Sometimes his favourite horse was killed and placed with all its harness in the ship. Occasionally, one or more of his female slaves would accompany their lord and were ceremonially strangled. Finally, the chief, his slaves and possessions were either burnt on a gigantic funeral pyre or were buried beneath a great mound of earth.

For a number of years, the Vikings were content to raid and pillage the rich lands of Europe. Later, they became more ambitious and set up fortified headquarters on islands in the middle of great rivers. As a result they were unhindered by the perils of the North Sea in winter and were able to spend the whole year campaigning.

Gradually, as the years went by, fewer Scandinavians went raiding. Some even started to settle in the countries they had previously attacked and new stable kingdoms appeared in present-day Norway, Sweden and Denmark. Other western Europeans had greatly improved their defences and started to inflict heavy defeats upon their hated enemies. At last, the great days of the Norsemen were over.

Right: Viking longships silently sail towards a sleeping town as the raiders prepare for their swift, sharp attack.

Ships of the Dead

Above: Viking burial ships were found at Oseberg, Gokstad, and Tune in Norway.

Above: The Oseberg burial ship is the most beautiful to have been excavated so far. However, **it had been badly damaged by subsidence and pressure from the earth above the ship.**

A number of Viking burial ships have been discovered and excavated. The most famous were found in Norway at Tune in 1867, Gokstad in 1880 and Oseberg in 1903. Each one had been buried beneath a great mound of earth.

The ship found at Oseberg was a beautiful vessel, some 21.5 metres long, 5 metres wide and 1.5 metres deep. It was a luxurious ship and was carefully decorated with carved wooden friezes. The bows ended in a snake's head. The stern was missing but probably had been carved in the shape of a snake's tail. In the days when it cut its way through high seas, it must have looked like a great sea-serpent with its timbers gleaming and its paintwork glistening.

The burial ship contained a large chamber amidships. Unfortunately, this had been broken into by thieves and many of its treasures had been stolen. The skeletons of two women were found nearby. The arms and hands of one of them had been badly damaged by the robbers when they ripped off her rings and gold bracelets. The other woman appeared to have lacked expensive ornaments (as her skeleton was intact) and she may have been a slave.

In spite of the robber's visit,

most of the ship's funeral furniture remained intact. There were two carved wooden beds with bedding, tapestries and chests for storing valuables. A complete kitchen was recovered consisting of casks, buckets, cauldrons, pots and cooking utensils (including a mill for grinding grain). There were vehicles, including a fine four-wheeled cart and four sleighs complete with riding harness. Four magnificent carved head-posts and some iron rattles completed the treasure. The head-posts were regarded as sacred while the rattles were probably used to frighten away evil spirits. Here and there in the ship, the excavating archaeologists found the remains of wheat, cress, apples, hazelnuts and walnuts. This food was intended to tide the women over until they reached the next world.

Such rich furniture would not have been provided for anyone less than a powerful queen. But who was she? The archaeologists had unearthed her skeleton, her ship and her goods but how could they find out her name and history?

Some archaeologists believe that the answers to these questions may lie in the *sagas* – ancient histories that were passed down from generation to generation by word of mouth and finally written down long after they had been composed. It may be that one of the skeletons belongs to the legendary Queen Asa described in a collection of ancient Icelandic sagas called the *Heimskringla* or *The Lives of the Norse Kings*.

According to the sagas, Asa was the beautiful young daughter of the king of Agdir. The elderly king of Vestfold, Gudrod the Hunting King, fell in love with her. When Asa refused to marry him, Gudrod attacked Agdir, killed Asa's father and brother, carried her off to his own land and forced her to marry him. About a year later, Asa gave birth to a healthy son who was named Halfdan.

Asa was determined to avenge her father and brother and waited patiently for a suitable opportunity. Gudrod began to drink more and more heavily and often returned to his longhouse in a state of near

collapse. Asa was able to persuade a servant to waylay and murder her husband one night as he staggered home. As soon as she was sure that her hated husband was dead, the triumphant queen sailed back to Agdir and claimed the throne for her infant son.

No one knows when Asa actually died but most historians think that it must have been in about the middle of the ninth century. Modern dating methods have shown that the Oseberg ship was buried in about A.D. 850. As Halfdan was an important Norwegian king who would have given his mother a splendid burial, and as there is no evidence that any other lady of similar fame and importance lived in Norway at this time, could it be that the name 'Oseberg' is a corruption of 'Asa's berg', which would have meant 'Asa's barrow'?

It is perfectly possible that Asa

and the buried queen are one and the same person, but this is by no means certain. The problem presented by the nameless skeleton is typical of many facing archaeologists. Very often such questions cannot be solved by research but only by detective work. Archaeologists study all the available evidence and then try to construct a logical answer to the problem facing them. But it is important to remember that many of these 'answers' are only theories, not facts.

Above: Most of the carefully reconstructed Oseberg ship is made of oak. Archaeologists believe that the ship had been laid up for some time before the burial. Even when it was new, the ship could not have been used for long journeys as it was too fragile.

Below: The Oseberg ship contained furniture, armour and food for use in the next world. This fine chest stored valuables and clothes.

Make a Viking Ship

The Vikings developed remarkable sailing vessels called longships. Each ship was very flexible, as its planks were only lashed, or tied, to a strong framework of ribs and crossbeams, instead of being nailed into place.

For several centuries, the ships were propelled only by oars, but by the seventh century the Vikings had learnt to fit them with masts and sails. The mast was erected amidships on a solid piece of wood called a mastfish and was held in position by ropes called stays or shrouds. Each ship had one large sail which was sewn on to a spar, or wooden crossbeam, and hoisted up the mast. The spar was raised or lowered to shorten or lengthen the sail. The longship was steered by a steerboard, a single large oar near the stern. On important occasions, such as entering port or on feast days, gaily coloured shields were attached to the ship's sides.

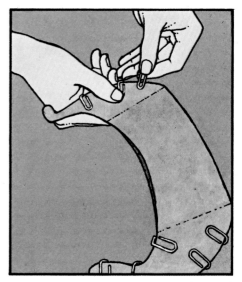

You will need: coloured manilla card, scissors, a ruler, a pencil, glue, graph paper, paper fasteners and clips, a 20 cm dowelling rod.

1. Copy the outlines of the different parts of the ship onto the graph paper, using the diagram below as a guide. Cut them out to make templates for the model.

2. Fold a piece of dark manilla card in half. Place template **A** on the card and draw round it. Cut out two pieces, which will form the hull of the ship. Fold the card along the dotted lines and glue the shaded areas. Join the two pieces of card and hold them together with paper clips until the glue is dry.

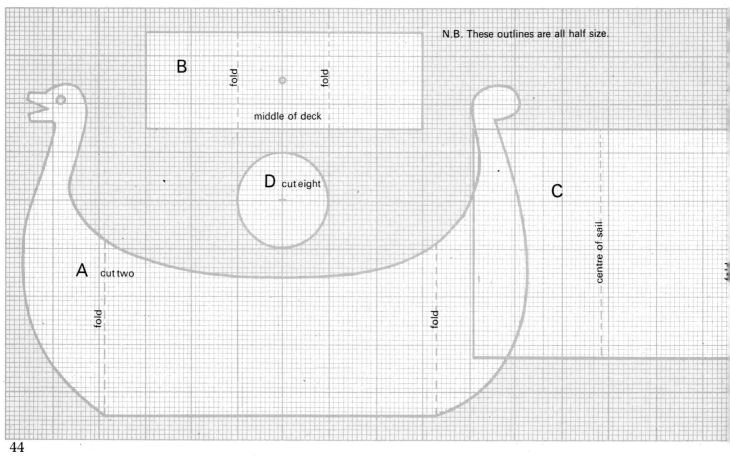

N.B. These outlines are all half size.

B

fold

fold

middle of deck

D cut eight

A cut two

fold

fold

C

centre of sail

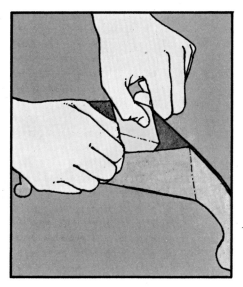 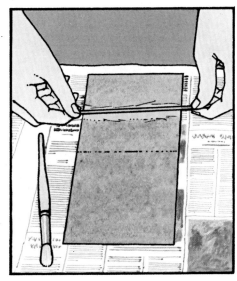 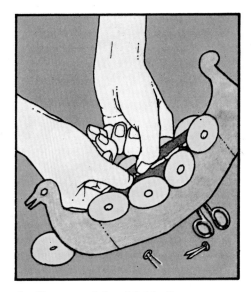

3. Cut out the deck from manilla card using template **B** as a guide. Make a small hole in the middle of the deck (as marked). Fold the card into three equal pieces and glue both end sections. Carefully slide the deck into place in the middle of the hull. Press the glued sections firmly against the ship's sides. Leave to dry.

4. Fold a piece of light manilla card in half. Using template **C**, cut out the double sail. Decorate the sail with strips of contrasting card. Glue about 13 cm of the dowelling rod and place in the centre of the sail. Glue together both halves of the sail. Leave to dry.

5. Cut out eight shields from manilla card, using template **D** as a guide. Make a hole through the centre of each shield. Fit them in place on the side of the ship with paper fasteners.

6. Set up the sail by pushing the dowelling mast through the hole in the deck to complete your ship.

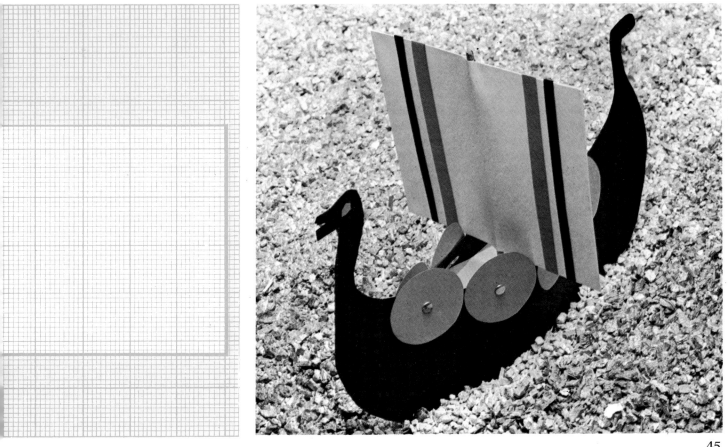

The Mountain Kingdoms

In 1536, a tough Spanish soldier called Gonzalo de Quesada set off with 600 soldiers and 85 horses to conquer a mysterious and wealthy civilization high in the Andes Mountains of South America. He had heard that the king of this land, El Dorado, the Gilded One, powdered himself with gold dust before throwing an offering of gold into a sacred lake. Fired by greed for gold and glory, the Spaniards slowly hacked their way through dense tropical forests and waded across treacherous swamps until they reached the great plains of the interior. Here, they were set upon by hordes of naked savages and fierce cannibals who shot them down with poisoned arrows.

Eventually, the Spaniards reached the slopes of the snow-crested Andes. By this time, all but 200 men had died of disease or starvation, had been eaten alive by jaguars and alligators, or had died from wounds caused by the poisoned arrows. On reaching the rich mountain valleys belonging to the Chibcha, or Muisca, tribes the Spaniards found a civilized people very different from the savages who had caused them such difficulties as they crossed the plains.

The peaceful Chibcha tribes formed two major states ruled by the Zipa kings of Bogotá and the Zaque chiefs of Tunja, in Colombia. They were a farming people who grew maize, potatoes and quinoa (a plant whose seeds the Indians made into cakes). Their largest city, Bogotá, contained 20,000 houses with mud and cane walls and thatched roofs. The Indian nobles and kings wore head-dresses decorated with gold and precious stones, gold jewellery, and finely worked gold breastplates. Their gods were fierce and, through the priests, demanded gifts of gold, incense, emeralds and corn. The sun-god was the most important and it was to him that El Dorado made the most spectacular offering of all.

At the beginning of his reign, each Zipa king made his way to Lake Guatavita. Just before dawn, he and his nobles went on board a specially-built raft and were rowed out into the lake. There, the king was stripped of his robes and finery, and had his body anointed with oil and gold dust. As the morning sun rose above the mountains overlooking the lake, the young king stood up among his nobles and allowed the sunshine to transform his glistening body to a blazing figure. Stepping swiftly to the end of the raft, he picked up handfuls of gold and emeralds from a great pile in the centre of the raft and hurled them into the sacred lake. In a few moments a fortune had been offered to the sun-god. King after king had performed this ceremony and an incalculable treasure of gold and emeralds had sunk to the bottom.

The arrival of the Spaniards, mounted on horseback, terrified the Chibcha people. The tribes fell back on all sides and allowed the Spaniards to do what they liked. In August 1537, Quesada marched to Tunja, burst into the city and seized the frightened king. The delighted Spaniards rushed through the deserted streets collecting the sheets of gold which hung tinkling in the wind outside the doors of the houses. Next, Quesada attacked Bogotá and killed its king in a skirmish. However, he discovered to his fury that the royal treasure had been smuggled out of the palace and hidden secretly somewhere in the jungle. Even though a number of Indians were cruelly tortured by the Spaniards, they did not reveal its whereabouts.

Soon, the great cities of the Chibcha were reduced to dust and their civilization destroyed. Their conquerors were the first of many treasure-hunters who found that the Chibcha treasure could be recovered only with difficulty and suffering.

Right: As the sun rises, El Dorado is rowed to the centre of Lake Guatavita on a specially constructed raft.

46

The Search for El Dorado

Above: El Dorado was the chief of the Chibcha people who lived in the northernmost part of the Andes around modern Bogatá.

From the time when the Spaniards first heard about El Dorado, they dreamed of recovering the treasure offered by him to the sun-god. As early as the 1550s, an explorer called Cieza de Leon suggested draining Lake Guatavita. The first person to attempt to do this was Gonzalo de Quesada's second-in-command, Lázaro Fonte. He had little success, however, and soon gave up. Later, Quesada's brother, Hernán, returned to the idea. He collected together large numbers of Indians who tried to lower the level of the lake by passing buckets of water from hand to hand until the water could be thrown away without draining back into the lake. After three months' labour, the lake was lowered by a few metres, and Hernán is said to have recovered about 3000 pesos worth of gold. Realizing that he would never achieve his objective in this way Hernán Quesada gave up in despair.

The most ambitious attempt to drain the lake was made by a Spanish merchant called Antonio de Sepúlveda in the 16th century. Having organized a vast labour force of 8000 Indians, he cut a great notch in the rim of the lake. At first it seemed that this operation would succeed as the lake was lowered by some 20 metres. Then, disaster struck. The great trench collapsed (killing many of the workers) and the water drained back into the lake. This catastrophe brought the attempt to an end and Sepúlveda died in poverty, even though he had found gold breastplates, gold eagles and serpents and a huge emerald.

Although other attempts were made to discover El Dorado's treasure between the 17th and the 19th centuries, few records mention them and probably little of value was discovered. Interest did not revive until 1801, when a very famous traveller and writer, Alexander von Humboldt, visited the lake and later calculated that there could be treasure then worth 300 million dollars lying at the bottom of Lake Guatavita.

In 1823, José Ignacio Paris founded a company to drain the lake. Shortly afterwards, a British naval captain called Charles Stuart Cochrane arrived and suggested building a canal to carry off the water. He became so interested that he decided to stay and supervise the work. On his orders, the sweating

Above: Lake Guatavita was one of the Chibcha people's sacred places. In the 16th century the Spaniards heard about the legendary El Dorado, who threw huge quantities of gold and jewels into a lake. As a result they spent many years searching for the lake.

labourers dug a great trench in the side of the lake. Unfortunately, the walls of the canal collapsed as the first water swirled through it. Cochrane excavated several more trenches, but with little success. The lake was lowered by about five metres, but this was not enough to enable the exhausted workers to reach the submerged treasure. Eventually, the merchants who provided the money for the project lost interest and the work stopped.

However, greed for gold caused another group of businessmen to set up a company called Contractors Ltd in 1899. They were joined by a brilliant engineer called Hernando de Villa who succeeded in draining the lake by digging an underground tunnel up through its bed. At last,

the great moment had arrived. Disappointment soon followed, however, as the workmen floundered around in the thick gluey mud without being able to reach the treasures. Worse was to come as the burning sun soon made the mud as hard as concrete. The treasure – if treasure there was – remained entombed in a layer of sun-dried brick. Gradually, the lake filled up, and the contractors realized that a different approach would have to be found. However, by now they had neither the necessary interest nor the money and, once again, Lake Guatavita was abandoned.

Marine divers tried their luck in 1932, but were defeated by the thick mud on the bottom of the lake. In 1953, after several more equally unsuccessful attempts, another marine engineer, called Timperly, dragged a steel ball equipped with movable claws along the lake bottom but once again without success. Although other companies and private fortune-seekers have tried to reach the treasure since, the sacred lake has stubbornly refused to yield up its secrets.

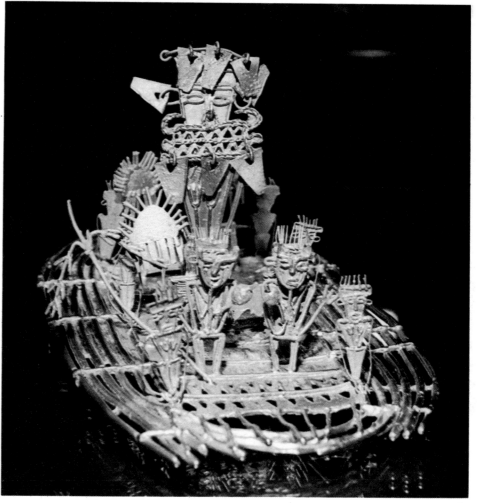

Colombian Gold

In some parts of Colombia, Indians had been making gold ornaments for more than 1000 years before the Spaniards arrived. Most of the Chibcha treasures were discovered by collectors or treasure-hunters who did not keep accurate records about which items were found together. They also ignored apparently valueless items of pottery which might have helped in dating finds. As a result, it is often difficult to date certain objects.

In such circumstances people use *typology* to date an object. This entails arranging and classifying finds according to their style. For example, archaeologists have identified four major Colombian styles, those of Tairona, Sinu, Muisca and Nariño. Each style can be divided into Early, Middle and Late periods, marked by developments in the Indians' techniques of design and metalwork. However, a great deal of Colombian gold work does not fit into this scheme and cannot yet be dated.

Above: A Colombian warrior's gold helmet decorated with feathers, a beautiful face mask, earrings, necklaces and a large round chest plate.

50

Make a golden mask

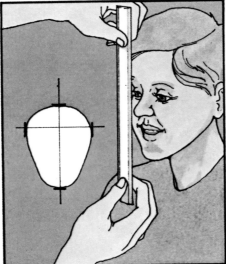

You will need: newspaper, wallpaper paste, plasticine, petroleum jelly, scissors, elastic thread, a bowl, gold paint, cardboard, a ruler, a pencil.

1. Get a friend to measure your face, so that the mask will fit. This drawing shows which measurements you need to know.

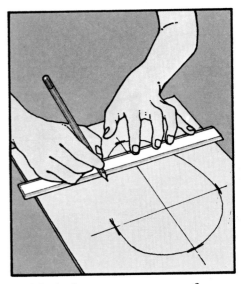

2. Mark the measurements of your face on the cardboard. Use them to help you draw the shape of your face on the cardboard. Ask an adult to help if you find this too difficult.

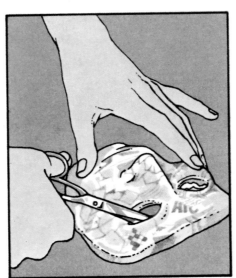

6. Gently ease the mask off the plasticine base. Cut away the papier mâché at the eyes (so that you will be able to see where you are going) and mouth. Trim around the edge of the mask to cut off any ragged edges.

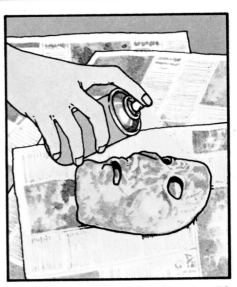

7. Paint the mask with gold paint. If you are using paint from a spray can, put the mask in the centre of several sheets of newspaper. This will make sure that you paint nothing but the mask!

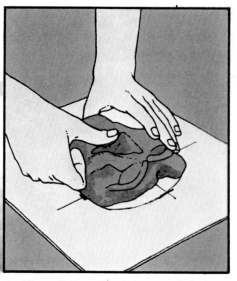

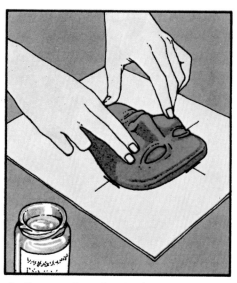

3. Knead the plasticine until it is soft. Fill in the outline on the board with plasticine and build it up to make the shape of the face. Make hollows for the eyes and mouth and add any areas of raised decoration.

4. Smear the plasticine with some petroleum jelly so that the papier mâché will not stick to it. Tear the newspaper into strips. Mix the wallpaper paste in the bowl until it is really smooth.

5. Paste strips of torn newspaper on each side and lay them in the same direction across the plasticine base. Go on papering in alternate directions until you have at least six layers on the base. Leave the mask to dry for three days so that it is really hard.

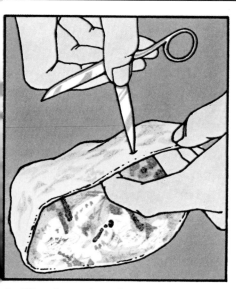

8. Use the point of a pair of scissors to make a small hole at about eye-level near either side of the mask. Ask an adult to help with this.

9. Thread a piece of elastic through both holes. Make sure that it will stretch around the back of your head. Tie a knot at each end and your mask is now complete.

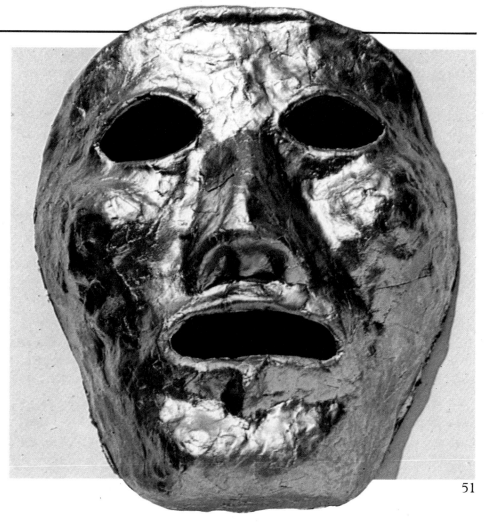

51

The First Emperor

Chün Wei, the captain of the Imperial Guard sighed and shook his head. To think that the reign of Shih Huang Ti of the Ch'in dynasty, the first emperor of all China, should end like this. Chün Wei's weary soldiers were toiling across the rolling northern plains of China in the boiling sun. In front, the emperor's great golden coach rocked crazily as it crossed the uneven ground. But to the soldiers' astonishment no roars of rage came from within. Chün Wei could guess what they were thinking. What could be wrong? Why had that waggon of stinking fish been placed behind the imperial coach? Why were the ministers so silent? The whole thing was a mystery. Only Chün Wei and the ministers knew the truth – that the emperor was dead. This secret was to be kept until the crafty ministers were sure that they would have control over the next emperor, Erh-Shih Huang Ti. The waggon-load of fish was merely to conceal the stench of the emperor's rotting body.

Chün Wei had been with Shih Huang Ti from the beginning. He had watched him when he was no more than a mere overlord of a single state ruthlessly destroying his rivals. In 221 B.C., for the first time in its history, all China had been united under one ruler.

What wonders Shih Huang Ti had performed. He had driven the Mongolian invaders out of northern China and had continued the construction of an enormous border wall. The Great Wall, as it was now known, defended 450 miles of the northern frontier. To consolidate his power, he had linked the beautiful capital, Hsien-yang, with the rest of the empire by a superb network of roads. He also joined together China's rivers with a series of canals to make the greatest waterways system in the ancient world. Under Shih Huang Ti's guidance, wasteland was reclaimed for the cultivation of crops, watered by a complex irrigation system. But

there was still unrest among the people.

Many nobles remained disloyal and jealous of Shih Huang Ti's power. Chün Wei remembered how he had helped to move some of the wealthy and powerful families to the capital where his master could keep his eagle eye on them. For years he had lived in constant fear of assassination and each day had moved restlessly from place to place in order to confuse his enemies.

Shih Huang Ti was especially wary of the scholars. He always feared that they would stir up the people against him. However, those who had stood in his way had paid heavily for their disloyalty. Chün Wei had arrested hundreds of them and helped statesman Li Ssu to burn thousands of books. Then they had had the satisfaction of burying 460 of the traitors alive.

Chün Wei had to admit that the last few years had been difficult. As his ambitious ministers fought for more power, the old emperor had become increasingly suspicious and touchy. Soon, even his friends did not dare to come near him. Instead, Shih Huang Ti had surrounded himself with doctors and magicians. He had become terrified of dying and had sent servants all over the world in search of the secret of everlasting life.

Now it was over. Who would fill the great man's shoes? By low tricks and deception the greedy ministers had arranged the death of the emperor's elder son. Now they hoped to rule through his spineless younger son. But Chün Wei would serve his master's family to the last. As soon as the huge imperial tomb had been sealed, he would unsheath his sword and cut down those who had preyed upon his master during his last days.

Right: Despite the harsh weather, the construction of the Great Wall of China continues at the Emperor's command.

52

A Ghostly Army

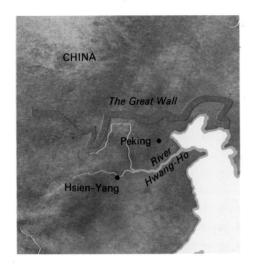

Above: The first emperor's capital, Hsien-yang, was on a bend of the Hwang-Ho river.

Shih Huang Ti of the Ch'in dynasty spent 38 years planning and constructing an enormous subterranean palace in which to spend eternity. According to Ssu-ma Chien, an early Chinese historian, the emperor employed 700,000 men to excavate the huge shaft and to pour the bronze foundations. Rare and beautiful objects made of jade, pearl, bronze, silk and linen, pottery and jewels were collected from all over Shih Huang Ti's empire and stored in this tomb. Craftsmen made mechanical crossbows, designed to shoot any thief entering the tomb.

After Shih Huang Ti's burial, it is said, the jade door of the tomb was sealed before the pallbearers had left the burial chamber. The emperor's son was afraid that they would return and loot his father's grave. The vast vault was then covered with a huge mound of earth and planted with trees, bushes, grass and flowers in an effort to disguise its whereabouts. Although this great mound was originally 166 metres high, it now stands only 34 metres above the surrounding countryside.

It was not until recently that archaeologists were able to excavate Shih Huang Ti's tomb. Indeed, the stories about it were all but

54

forgotten. Then, in 1974, some peasants from the Hsien-yang village commune in Shensi province were working in their fields when they unearthed some curious life-size painted *terracotta* figures. Soon a team of Chinese archaeologists was probing the whole area. To their astonishment, they discovered literally hundreds of these figures. More than 500 pottery soldiers still carrying real swords, spears and crossbows have since been recovered.

Over 24 magnificent pottery horses have also been unearthed. The horses, which are arranged in groups of four, are superbly modelled with tossing heads and flaring nostrils. Each group is drawing a real chariot with leather harness and bronze fastenings. The chariots contain models of charioteers, spearmen and archers.

What was the purpose of this ghostly army? In the days of the Shang, the earliest Chinese rulers (1700-1100 B.C.), real warriors, servants and horses were buried alive with kings and high-ranking officials. Any of a ruler's wives who had not borne children were buried with him so that they could provide him with sons and daughters in the next world. Although this practice had been given up long before Shih Huang Ti's death in 210 B.C., he went as close as he dared to reviving the old custom. He was determined to take not only his treasures but also his army with him to the next world.

Although only a small part of this city of the dead has been exposed, it is calculated that it contains statues of at least 600 fully-armed soldiers. Chinese archaeologists believe that this huge ghostly army was originally buried in a vast vault extending over more than 12,500 square metres and that the roof later collapsed leaving the soldiers

Right: The heads of three terracotta figures buried at Hsien-yang.

Right: One of Shih Huang Ti's soldiers in full regalia.

Above: A magnificent pottery horse representing one of the emperor's living animals.

waiting to be discovered centuries later.

When the archaeologists looked carefully at the figures, they were filled with admiration. No two of them are the same. It seems likely that the all-powerful emperor ordered his artists to produce portrait statues of his favourite guards and horses. Each of the life-size soldiers depicts a different man. Some bear fierce, proud expressions; others appear to be smiling gently.

All this information has been obtained from excavating only one section of the great vault. What wonders may be awaiting the archaeologists in the burial chamber itself? Work has now begun on excavating Shih Huang Ti's capital city of Hsien-yang. The foundations of many great palaces, mighty walls of rammed earth, luxurious dwellings and a fine drainage system have already been uncovered. These discoveries and the remarkable finds in Shih Huang Ti's tomb show that the stories about him have not been exaggerated; he was not only China's first emperor but also one of its greatest.

55

Make a Chinese Soldier

The peasants who unearthed the first terracotta fragments at Hsien-yang in 1974 could have never dreamed of making such an amazing discovery. The life-size pottery army is remarkable, both because the figures are unusually well-preserved and because each one is unique.

The emperor Shih Huang Ti obviously wanted to be buried with replicas of the people who had served him during his lifetime, as he did not dare to revive the traditional Chinese practice of live burials. His servants and soldiers must have been happy to pose while artists modelled each person's features, knowing that the terracotta figures would be buried in their place.

As archaeologists now estimate that there may be as many as 6000 figures in the tomb, they may well have taken one or two artists almost a lifetime to construct.

You will need: clay, a rolling pin, a modelling tool, a knife, newspaper, a dowelling rod, paper, a pencil, scissors, a small sponge.

1. Cover your work surface with newspaper, so that you do not make a mess.

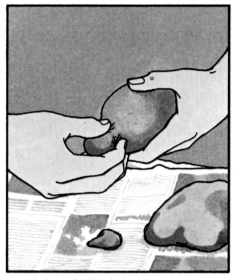

2. Make a ball of clay, about the size of a tennis ball, by patting the clay in the palm of your hands. Place the clay on the newspaper. Gently squeeze out some clay between your fingers to make the shape of the head, leaving enough clay to form the soldier's body.

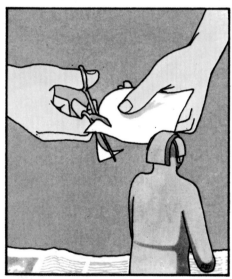

6. Work out the details of the clothes (leggings and a tunic) and armour (a breast plate) on paper. The shapes you will need are shown on the next page. Cut out patterns, or templates, from paper or thin card to the right size to fit the body of the model.

7. Roll out a thin sheet of clay. Place the templates on the clay and draw around them. Cut out the clay and carefully fit the skirt, then the tunic and, finally, the armour to the body. Use your fingers and the modelling tool to complete the head of the model.

8. Carefully, cover the model with a polythene bag, so that it will dry slowly without cracking. Leave it to dry out in a safe place, then lift the model off the dowelling support.

9. You can paint the finished model or leave the clay undecorated, just like the real pottery soldiers.

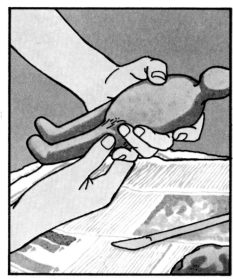
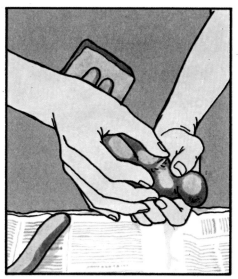

3. Roll out two sausages of clay to make the soldier's legs. Join them to the body with small coils of clay. Smooth the joins until they cannot be seen. Roll out a thick slab of clay. Join this to the feet of the model to make a steady base. Do not try to stand up the figure yet.

4. Roll out two slightly smaller sausages of clay to make the soldier's arms. Join these to the body in the same way as the legs. Leave the clay to dry out slightly as it will still be very soft.

5. Carefully insert the dowelling rod through the base and into the centre of the figure. Stick the other end into a block of clay. Now you can work on the model standing up. Use your fingers and a modelling tool to finish off the feet and hands of the model.

Armour template patterns

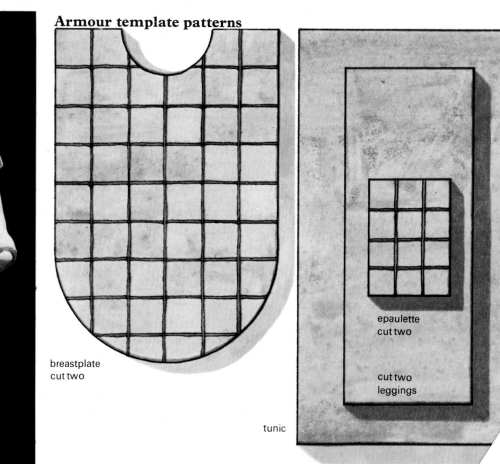

breastplate
cut two

epaulette
cut two

cut two
leggings

tunic

A Byzantine Shipwreck

As the merchant ship *The Argos* pulled out of Constantinople harbour, Captain Georgios looked about with satisfaction. He never grew tired of the splendid view. Through the vast forest of ships' masts he could see an imperial galley making its way across the harbour. The sound of rhythmic drumming came across the water as the oarmaster beat time for the galley slaves whose oars dipped into and lifted out of the water in unison.

Georgios turned to look at the magnificent city of Constantinople. It was the seventh century A.D. and the hills were dotted with elegant palaces and churches. In the *hippodrome*, vast crowds would be watching the races and betting their last coin on their favourite horse. If things followed their usual course, the meeting would end in rioting.

Once outside the harbour, the little craft caught the wind and was soon bowling along. The crew, about a dozen sailors and a carpenter, were chatting and joking among themselves. Georgios had bought a consignment of wine jars straight from the potteries and his men were waterproofing them with resin. His men needed something useful to do on the long voyage to the island of Kos near south-eastern Asia Minor, as bored sailors soon began quarrelling. This way, Georgios increased his profit and kept his men busy.

The sound of boisterous singing coming from the galley reminded him that it was not long to supper. Some mussels, fresh bread and a bowl of the cook's excellent stew washed down with good wine would keep everybody happy until morning. Pacing the deck, the captain noticed that the sails were sagging and ordered the helmsmen to keep closer to the wind.

The sun set slowly, staining the sea and the sky a brilliant red. Soon, the ship was sailing along by the cold light of the moon. There was little danger of shipwreck as the shore was clearly marked by a white line of breaking waves. In the morning, the breeze strengthened and the little vessel made fine time crossing the Sea of Marmara. The next day, they passed through the Dardanelles to the Aegean Sea.

By dusk Georgios was in good spirits. The voyage was already half over and many wine jars were ready to sell. In another day they would arrive at Kos. With luck he would be able to sell his cargo, take on board a consignment of wine, and be home within a week.

While he stood daydreaming, towering black clouds appeared on the horizon and before long had blotted out the sun. With the clouds came gale-force winds which sent *The Argos* pitching and plunging through rapidly rising seas. The wind quickly whipped the waves up into great walls of water which smashed down on the decks of the little ship. Sudden strong breezes were a common hazard, but Georgios quickly realized that this was no squall.

In the dim light, the captain ordered his frightened helmsmen to head for an island which he could see looming through the spray. Once in the lee of the island, they might be able to ride out the storm. Slowly, the small craft neared safety as the helmsmen and their mates battled with the huge rudder oars. Suddenly, a great gust of wind spun the vessel away like a twig in a stream and flung it towards the shore. The sailors struggled with the ropes but there was a terrible rending noise as hidden rocks tore out the bottom of the ship. One great wave poured over her and she was gone.

On the storm-tossed sea, there remained nothing but a few spars and the bobbing heads of the crew, who were desperately trying to stay afloat. Of *The Argos*, nothing more was to be seen.

Right: The helmsmen of *The Argos* struggle to keep her away from the rocks.

Underwater Archaeology

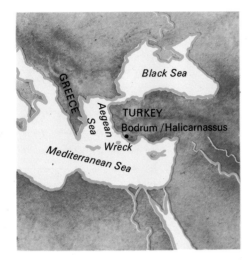

Above: A Byzantine merchant ship sank off the southern coast of Turkey in a fierce storm.

In A.D. 625 or 626, a Byzantine merchant ship sailing east along the coast of Asia Minor (modern Turkey) struck a reef some 20 miles from Halicarnassus and sank. The wreck was discovered by a diver in 1958 and the underwater site was excavated between 1961 and 1964.

The recovery work was carried out by expert divers wearing aqua suits and carrying aqualungs of air on their backs. Unfortunately, the wreck lay in more than 30 metres of water, where the pressure is so great that a diver can absorb too much nitrogen, lose consciousness and drown. If he comes to the surface too quickly, he can suffer the agonies of 'the bends' when paralysing bubbles form in the bloodstream. Swimmers in this condition die unless they can be placed in a *decompression chamber* where the air pressure can be reduced very slowly.

The archaeologists worked in remarkably the same way underwater as they would have done on dry land. The wreck was marked out by a *grid* made of scaffolding. Cameras and powerful lights were fixed to the scaffolding. All kinds of suction pumps (similar to high-powered vacuum cleaners) helped to remove the covering

layers of sand and mud. Finds were placed in wire baskets and hauled to the surface.

The sailing ship which the archaeologists restored timber by timber was a streamlined coaster, 19 metres long and five metres wide. The vessel had been powered by one or more sails on a single mast and steered by two enormous oars, one on each side of the hull towards the stern. A hatch between the steering oars and the mast gave access to the cargo hold. The craft must have been remarkably fast for a coaster, presumably so that it could outsail any pirate vessels.

The galley, or kitchen, which was situated at the stern, rose 80 centimetres above the deck and had a tiled roof. One tile had a cir ular hole pierced in it through which the smoke from the fire would have escaped. Inside the galley, there was a firebox made of tiles and iron bars, as well as 22 pots; two copper cauldrons; a large jar for fresh water; and assorted crockery. There were also some tools, including axes and shovels, which were probably used by landing parties looking for firewood and fresh water.

After recovering all these artefacts, the archaeologists started to ask many questions. Who had owned the ship? It seems that the owner and captain was probably a

Above: Divers prepare to search for buried treasure. A small engine provides power for the pumping and lifting equipment used to raise artefacts from the seabed.

Below: Beneath the Mediterranean Sea are hundreds of wrecks. This diver has found a remarkably well-preserved amphora.

Greek called Georgios whose name and title were carved on the ship's expensive weighing scales. What kind of crew would he have had? According to a Byzantine law book, such a vessel would have had a cook, a carpenter and several crewmen. The presence of a carpenter was proved by the recovery of a workbox containing hammers, chisels, punches, files and drill-bits. Apart from the cook, there was little evidence of the rest of the crew.

What was the ship carrying? About 900 *amphorae* or storage jars of various sizes were found on board. Some were lined with resin which was the customary method of waterproofing in those days. The presence of a pot of congealed resin suggests that the crew were treating the amphorae during the voyage.

Where did the ship come from? Constantinople (modern Istanbul) or one of the nearby towns was probably its home port. The ship's lamps and pottery all came from the area around Constantinople.

Where was the ship going? As it was carrying wine jars, it is reasonable to assume that the ship was making for either Kos, Knidos or Rhodes, which were celebrated wine-producing islands in the Aegean and Mediterranean Seas.

When was the ship wrecked? 70 coins were discovered in the wreck. Only two had been minted before the reign of the Emperor Heraclius (A.D. 610–41) and the latest minted in A.D. 625. It can therefore be assumed that the ship sank soon after the last coin was issued.

Thus all these questions were answered by studying the fragments of pottery, wood and metal recovered from the seabed and by the use of common sense. The wreck was like a jigsaw. Slowly, the archaeologists fitted together the pieces and completed the picture to provide a valuable insight into the way of life aboard a seventh-century Mediterranean merchant ship.

Above: This diver is about to rest in a decompression chamber. In this way he can stay underwater longer when swimming in deep water.

Below: Archaeologists often find artefacts strewn in pieces all over the seabed. However, this amphora seems to have suffered little damage.

61

Be an Underwater Detective

Underwater archaeology is one of the newest and most exciting of archaeological techniques. It requires a combination of all the traditional archaeological methods, and modern diving skills.

As with most archaeological finds, ruins and artefacts are usually buried, broken into fragments and scattered. As a result, divers often have difficulty both in locating objects beneath layers of sand and mud and in raising the finds to the surface, where the archaeologists can begin the task of identification.

Be an underwater detective

1. Can you guess what this diver is using to scan the seabed?

2. This diver is 'hoovering' the seabed. What do you think happens to the debris which is sucked up to the surface?

3. Can you guess what this diver is doing?

4. This diver is sketching part of the wreck. How do you think he can do this underwater?

5. What do you think this is?

6. Why is this diver able to remove his mask in the diving bell?

Answers

1. The diver is using a metal detector. It has a dial to show when metal has been found.
2. The debris is sieved, so that no small objects of archaeological significance are overlooked.
3. The diver is using a special underwater camera to photograph a square on the grid to record the wreck exactly as it was first found.
4. He uses a waterproof crayon and writes on sheets of white plastic.
5. It is a balloon lift. When the basket is full the bag is filled with air and floats to the surface.
6. He can breathe air which is pumped down from the surface.

Right: This site has a grid and is similar to one on dry land.

The Outpost

Marcus Sextus lifted his helmet and mopped his forehead. He found it unbelievably hot even though he had been born and brought up in southern Italy. Italian summers were mild compared with the parching heat of the Syrian desert. The *centurion* shaded his eyes and peered out over the endless waste of rock, sand and wizened bushes to the horizon.

What a location for his last posting, he thought a little bitterly: a lonely outpost on the Empire's uneasiest frontier. In the third century A.D. the Romans and Persians were struggling for control of this no man's land. They had both plunged deep into the desert but it still remained the frontier.

The little fort seemed to doze in the blazing heat. Marcus could hear his sentries marching up and down with measured tread and the crunch of their heavy studded boots as they turned about. Hot salty sweat would be running down their faces and necks. Their bronze *cuirasses* or breast-plates would be rubbing painfully against their shoulders while their heavy swords slapped against their thighs. Every so often they would briefly relax their hold on the handgrip of their great rectangular shields.

Most of the garrison were veterans like Marcus. They had served all over the western world: Spain, France, Greece, North Africa, even Britain. Their hard sunburnt faces bore witness to service on many a frontier. Glancing down, Marcus felt the stirrings of pride as his eyes caught sight of the battered bracelet of honour clasped about his wrist. He had won that at some cost, dragging an injured soldier from under a chariot and holding off the wild British tribesmen until help arrived.

A trumpet sounded. It was noon. Time to inspect the new guard and dismiss the old. Below him, he heard the bellowed orders of Aurelius, his second-in-command, and the sound of running feet.

Marcus slowly descended the steps from the watchtower by the main gate, giving the soldiers time to settle down. Straightening his back and twitching his armour into place, he strode out into the white hot glare of the sun. Instantly, he felt perspiration break out all over his body. He paced along the line of *legionaries*, checking every article of equipment, pointing out a flap here and a buckle there that was not quite in place. To his men he was just and fair but tough.

The inspection completed, Marcus returned to the top of the watchtower. Satisfied that nothing was moving on the horizon, he cast a critical eye over the garrison. The straight roads leading from the main square to the fort's four gateways and the barracks looked neat enough for any inspection.

Satisfied, Marcus walked down the steps and made his way to his quarters for a light lunch: some bread, cheese and a little fruit washed down by a glass or two of red wine. Hunger appeased, he lay down on his bed and enjoyed a short *siesta*. After an hour's sleep, he walked to the baths where he stripped, scraped the dirt from his body with a *strigil*, or blunt-edged knife, and wallowed in the warm bath for half an hour. After a quick plunge into the cold bath, he was massaged and oiled by his servant.

Later, when the sun had gone down, Marcus joined his fellow centurions for a meal. It was soon time for him to inspect the night guard, and to go on his rounds. Looking over the empty desert by the light of the moon, Marcus again began to dream about his native Italy. He smiled as he thought of his retirement when he would return there and leave behind the scorching heat and dull routine of the Syrian desert garrison.

Right: Centurion Marcus Sextus inspects the new guard at a lonely desert outpost as part of his routine duties.

Archæology from the Air

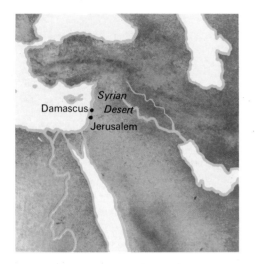

Above: A series of Roman forts were built in the Syrian desert.

The biplane banked slowly while Lieutenant-Colonel Beazeley of the British Army carefully studied the Syrian desert below for any signs of Turkish troop movements. There was nothing to be seen. Suddenly, something unusual caught his eye. Indicating which way he wanted his pilot to fly, Beazeley leant out of the cockpit. There below lay the perfect plan of a Roman fort, the hidden remains of its walls and the buildings surrounding a central square were clearly outlined in the sand below. Realizing that this could be an important find, Beazeley quickly took a photograph of the scene below him.

Left: Alexander Keiller was a leading flier in the 1920s. He and O. G. S. Crawford were two of the earliest Englishmen to employ air photography as an archaeological tool.

Below: A series of ring ditches at Abingdon in England is revealed by crop marks in this aerial photograph. There are many prehistoric remains in this area, including an early causeway camp.

Unfortunately, soon afterwards, he was shot down and captured so that he was not able to publish the news of his discovery until after the First World War was over in 1918.

Although there had been early experiments, which involved taking photographs from hot-air balloons, aerial photography as an archaeological tool had not really come into its own until the First World War (1914–18). During the Middle Eastern battle campaign members of the British, French and German forces (such as Lieutenant-Colonel Beazeley) took aerial photographs. Initially designed to show enemy troop movements, some of these later proved to be of the greatest archaeological interest. Léon Rey, a Frenchman, used air photographs taken on campaign to reveal ancient remains in Macedonia (later part of Greece) in 1916. Later, a German called Theodor Wiegand was posted to his country's forces specifically in order to help protect historical monuments in Palestine and the Sinai Desert. He was able to photograph archaeological sites and to report on his findings.

Further progress was made in the 1920s. In 1922, a British R.A.F. officer, Air Commodore Clark-Hall, started to take aerial photographs of many parts of Hampshire in England. He showed these to an archaeologist called Crawford who was able to identify the outlines of many prehistoric fields lying beneath modern ones. Inspired by these finds, Crawford took many more aerial photographs which led to the discovery of a number of sites containing prehistoric hilltop camps and temples which had once resembled Stonehenge. Meanwhile, a famous French aviator, Father Antoine Poidebard, had taken a series of photographs of the Syrian desert which enabled historians to trace the outlines of many Roman and Arab fortifications. The sand which hid the sites from ground level was like glass from the air.

The Second World War (1939–45) saw tremendous developments in the technique and quality of aerial photography. Aeroplanes belonging to both sides flew over enemy territory photographing the countryside in an effort to discover military installations. As the interpretation of air photographs is a very difficult art, many archaeologists were employed by the armed forces as photographic intelligence officers.

Since the Second World War, air photography has become a major means of archaeological investigation and recording. Now all archaeologists have to be expert in their interpretation. Why is it that ruins and boundaries that cannot be seen at ground level appear on air photographs? In the early morning or late in the afternoon, when the sun is low in the sky, any remains cast long shadows, which can be observed clearly and recorded on film.

Archaeological sites lying under fields of corn or tea-plants show up on air photographs taken in the spring. Crops growing over buried ruins are usually shorter than those growing on deep soil, and, due to the richness and depth of topsoil, crops growing over buried ditches are usually taller. These tell-tale signs, known as crop marks, are only visible in ripening crops, as the plants have usually grown to the same height by harvest.

In many countries, governments are attempting to build up a complete photographic record of their country from the air. This helps them not only to produce really accurate maps of the area but also to discover a great deal about ancient roads, fields, buildings and settlements. In Europe and North America most of this work has already been done but elsewhere, no doubt, archaeologists using this technique will still make many more exciting discoveries.

Below: In this aerial photograph, the outline of an 18th-century house and its gardens are clearly defined.

Below: Remains of the Roman town of Silchester seen from the air. Markings which would hardly show on an ordinary

photograph stand out clearly, outlined in red and blue, on the infra-red false colour picture (right).

Aerial Interpretation

The use of aerial photography in archaeology is a great deal older than most people think. The first aerial photographs were taken from balloons in the second half of the 19th century, although the technique of aerial photography was not really mastered until well into the 20th century. It is now one of the archaeologists' most valuable modern tools.

Viewing archaeological sites from the air provides archaeologists with new information which may not be visible at ground level. It is sometimes very difficult to recognize the tell-tale signs of hidden ruins unless you have been carefully trained in interpreting aerial photographs. The following quiz is about aerial photography and *interpretation*. The photographs are fairly easy to understand, so see how much you can interpret.

Be an aerial archaeologist

1. Crop marks caused by variations in crop growth are one of the signs of ancient remains which an archaeologist will look for in an aerial photograph. The diagram above right shows a section through a field which would show crop marks if seen from high in the air. Can you guess why the plants at **A** are shorter than the rest? Why are the plants at **B** the tallest?

2. Even shadows can reveal hidden archaeological sites such as this ancient village and early field system (right). However, shadow sites are not visible all the time. At what time of day do you think this photograph must have been taken?

3. Although the round barrows in this photograph (far right, above) would be visible at ground level, the aerial view gives an accurate picture of the arrangement and number of the barrows. How many barrows can you count.

4. The outline of a Roman shore fort (below right) shows because of soil marks. Can you guess how soil marks are formed?

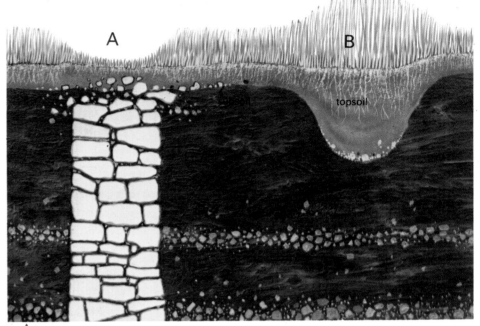

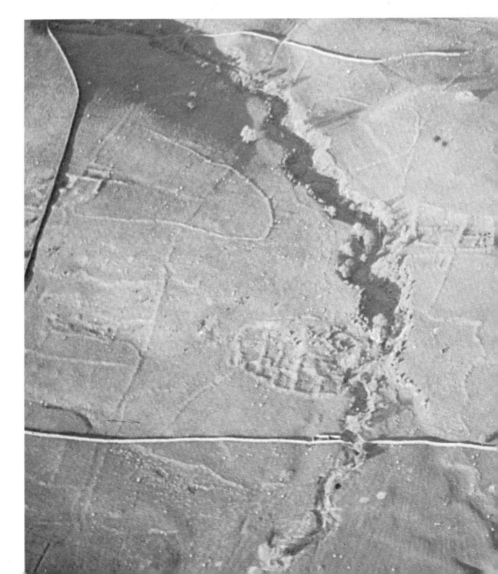

Below: An aerial photograph of Eller Beck in North Yorkshire, England. In the top right hand corner, now planted with a clump of trees, is a round barrow. **The remains of a Roman fort (in the centre of the photograph) show clearly as crop marks are picked out by the shadows.**

Above: These barrows are to be found at Lambourne, Berkshire in England. Barrows are circular or elongated prehistoric burial mounds.

Above: This fort at Brancaster was built by Romans to keep out the Saxon invaders. Its **square shape distinguishes it from inland, rectangular-shaped forts.**

Answers

1. The plants at **A** are shorter because they are growing over the hidden remains of a wall. The thin layer of topsoil means that the plants' roots cannot reach very deep into the earth and thus their growth is stunted. The plants at **B** are taller because of the deep ditch which has filled with rich topsoil.

2. This photograph must have been taken either very early or late in the day. When the sun is low in the sky, even slight mounds or hollows will cast long shadows.

3. At least 12 barrows can be seen in this picture.

4. Soil marks are formed when ancient remains are levelled. The contrasting colours such as crushed mud brick against chalky soil can be seen clearly from the air.

The Festival of the New Spears

All the boys huddled together in fear and anticipation. At last the moment had come. For years they had lived happily together in the boys' house learning how to handle their weapons: the flint knife, the spear and the sling. They had hunted, fished and learnt which fruits and roots were good to eat. During that time, they had grown tall and strong. Now it was time for the Festival of the New Spears which would mark their entry into manhood. What awaited them? Nobody would tell them about the sacred rites and no one had ever heard them mentioned. It was forbidden to speak of the ceremony.

The boys waited with increasing excitement for the great moment to arrive. Nobody was allowed to eat, but they sat and talked or dozed the long day through. Towards dusk the boys' instructor arrived to supervise them as they oiled their skins and smoothed back their hair.

As the sun slowly sank they were marched away from the village. Their mothers watched them go, smiling and crying at one and the same time. As the boys approached the Place of Life, their excitement became almost unbearable. For the first time in their lives, they were being allowed to pass into the holy of holies.

Before them, lit by firelight, was a wide forecourt containing some granite upright stones (already ancient in this year 2000 B.C.) decorated with green plants and flowers. Beyond the standing stones yawned the great black mouth of the enormous barrow, or burial mound, which towered above them. Filled with awe the boys stood and stared at the gigantic stone uprights which supported the lintel above the doorway. Beneath the great mound, it was said, the chiefs and heroes of the tribe slept for all time.

At a murmured command the men of the village stepped out of the shadows and lit their torches at the fire. Instantly, the whole scene was transformed. Looking about

70

them for their fathers and brothers, the boys shrank back with shock. Instead of friendly faces, they saw the masks of strangers whose bodies were painted all over with spirals, circles and triangles.

While the bewildered boys were still trying to recognize a friend or relative, a horn sounded. At the mouth of the barrow now stood the figure of a man wearing a mask and stag's antlers. As the flickering torchlight played on his body, the men let out a shout of welcome and beat their spears on the ground. This man was the high priest who was beloved of the spirits.

Then dancing began and everyone except the boys joined in what became a whirling mass of chanting figures. At last, the horn sounded again. The men stopped and stood silent. Richly dressed helpers led the boys one by one through the gaping mouth of the barrow, along the passage with its curiously carved wall, and into the sanctuary. Then their faces and bodies were painted, each in a different way, while the high priest revealed the sacred secrets of life.

As each boy rejoined his fellows in the forecourt he received his spear, the mark of his manhood, which showed he was now one of the New Spears. At last, the ceremony was complete and the men bellowed their approval as the high priest pointed to the New Spears. All eyes turned in their direction. When they looked back the high priest had disappeared.

As soon as the New and the Old Spears had removed all traces of the sacred paint, they returned to the village where the women had prepared a feast. The celebrations continued for the rest of the night and, in the morning, the New Spears moved into the men's house. Their new life had begun.

Right: Boys nervously wait for the masked priest to reveal the secrets of the warriors' life at the Festival of the New Spears.

The Carbon-14 Revolution

Above: Megalithic tombs have been found in the Orkney Islands and in western France.

In prehistoric times, festivals like that of the New Spears may have taken place all over western Europe. Certainly, archaeologists have been struck by the apparent similarity between the great stone or *megalithic* monuments of Europe. Until the 1940s, it was taken for granted that these monuments had been invented in the Mediterranean countries and that the idea had then been carried to other parts of Europe by traders or invaders. Tombs in Crete could be dated to about 2600 B.C. and it was therefore argued that similar tombs at Carnac in France must have been built in about 2000 B.C., while others in the Orkney Islands could not have been started before about 1800 B.C. However, the development of a new system of *chronology* has made archaeologists question this whole theory.

For many years the only way ancient cultures could be dated accurately was through the discovery of ancient histories containing a chronological list of kings. By this means historians were able to fix firm dates for events taking place in the countries of Mesopotamia and Egypt from about 3000 B.C. As it was believed that these civilizations were the most advanced in the ancient

Above: This passage grave at Maes Howe in the Orkneys is older than was once thought.

world, archaeologists took it for granted that the most important discoveries and inventions, such as the cultivation of wild cereals, the domestication of wild animals and the smelting of metals, were made in these areas and then spread west to Europe and east to parts of Asia. Then, in the 1940s, Dr Willard Libby introduced the radio-carbon dating system which eventually turned upside down many long-accepted theories.

He showed that all living things absorb a radioactive substance called carbon-14 from the air. From the moment of death the carbon-14 appeared to decay at a regular and measurable rate. Libby suggested that it obviously followed that bone, wood and other natural materials could be dated by measuring their carbon-14 content. After a time, however, it was discovered that the level of carbon-14 in the atmosphere was

Above: Part of an early carbon-14 dating machine. It reduces samples to gas.

Above: There are nearly 3000 prehistoric stone uprights at Carnac in western France.

Above: A section through a fossilized tree clearly showing growth rings.

not constant. As a result some archaeologists questioned whether this dating system was reliable.

Meanwhile an American, Dr C. W. Ferguson, had been studying tree-rings as a way of dating objects from the past. Gradually, he built up a continuous tree-ring 'calendar' dating back to 6100 B.C. It was then found possible to measure the carbon-14 content of each ring so that the variations in its rate of loss could be recorded. By comparing the tree-ring information with the results of carbon-14 tests, archaeologists believed that they could fix the exact date of objects originating from any time after 6100 B.C. This was an enormous breakthrough and has brought about the so-called 'carbon-14 dating revolution'.

By using these methods, the dating of the European megalithic monuments was stood on its head. It now appeared that the Orkney

tombs date from about 2500 B.C. and the French ones from 4200 B.C.. However, the Mediterranean tombs still dated from about 2600 B.C. What did this mean? Megalithic monuments could hardly have been introduced into western Europe by Mediterranean peoples thousands of years before they were building them themselves. Obviously, some European peoples had discovered how to build these monuments long before the apparently more 'civilized' Mediterranean nations. On looking at these monuments again, archaeologists became more aware of how much the tombs differ from each other. It seemed that the early archaeologists had exaggerated the similarities between early monuments and played down their differences because they believed that all the major inventions and discoveries had taken place in the Near East or in Mediterranean countries.

In the same way, this dating process has shown that some European peoples knew how to smelt metals long before the time suggested by the old textbooks. It has been proved, for instance, that 3000 years before the great days of the Greeks and Romans, European farmers had discovered how to smelt copper and gold. Even more important, it may mean that cattle and pigs were domesticated from early times in eastern Europe as well as in Turkey. In fact, it seems more likely that the cultivation of wild cereals, the domestication of animals and the smelting of metals happened independently in many different places all over the world at approximately the same period of time. As a result archaeologists have had to rethink many of their theories and change them for new ones.

Whatever else it has done, the carbon-14 revolution has presented archaeologists all over the world with a mass of completely new problems to solve.

Dates and Ages

The simplest way of measuring time is to count from a fixed date. In western countries the Christian calendar, so-called because the year of the birth of Jesus Christ is taken as the fixed date, is used for dating. All dates occurring after the birth of Christ have the letters 'A.D.' placed before them. A.D. stands for Anno Domini, which is Latin for 'the Year of Our Lord'. All dates occurring before the birth of Christ have the letters 'B.C.', which stand for Before Christ, placed after them.

People are sometimes confused when they have to work out dates from about the time of Christ or earlier. This is because the numbering of the years before the birth of Christ decreases, while the numbering of the years after the birth of Christ increases. This is shown most clearly on a simple date line such as the one drawn at the foot of the page.

A question of dates

See if you can work out the following problems involving dates. You can use the date line to help you. (The answers are at the foot of the next page.)

1. If a man was born in 70 B.C. and died in 32 B.C., how old was he at the time of his death?

2. The Roman emperor Caesar Augustus reigned from 30 B.C. to A.D. 14. How long did he rule?

3. If a 28 year-old woman died in A.D. 19, what was the year of her birth?

4. The building of the Pantheon in Rome began in 30 B.C. and took 154 years to complete. In what year was the building finished?

Right: A dateline spanning the years from 200 B.C. to A.D. 150. It shows some of the events which happened during this period.

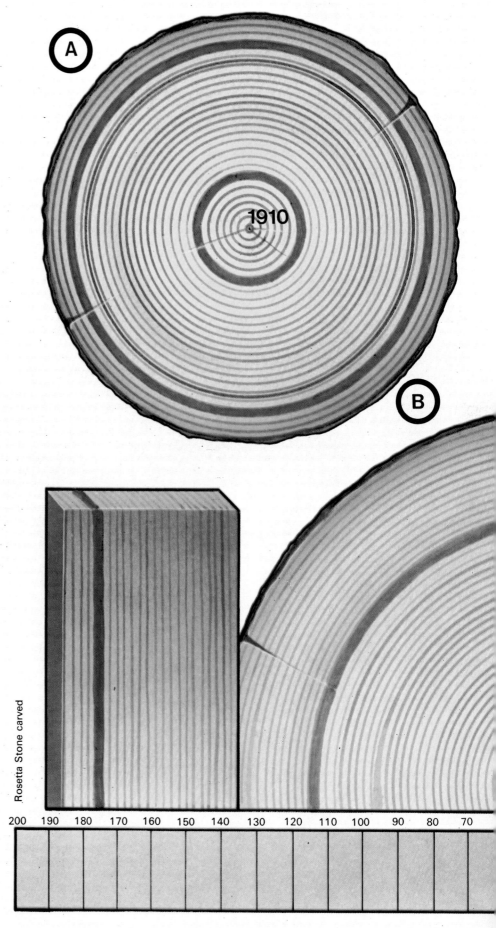

Rosetta Stone carved

200	190	180	170	160	150	140	130	120	110	100	90	80	70

Above: This section through a piece of timber shows the growth rings of the original tree. These differ in width depending on the amount of annual rainfall.

How old are these trees?

Each year a tree grows a ring of new wood, which is wider in a wet year than in a dry one. Trees which grow in the same climatic region therefore show similar tree-ring patterns when they are felled. If you study these tree-trunk sections carefully, and count the rings, you should be able to answer these questions.

1. Tree **A** was planted in 1910. When was it cut down?
2. Tree **B** was felled in 1930. When was it planted?
3. By looking at tree **A** can you tell in which years there was heavy rainfall?

How old is this timber?

The science of dendrochronology, or calculating dates by counting tree-rings, which proved so helpful in checking radio-carbon dating theories was discovered in the 1920s by an American called A. E. Douglas. He showed how tree-ring patterns could be matched with those of old timbers from the same region, thus providing a means of dating certain ancient remains.

To date archaeological material by dendrochronology you need a master plan or tree-ring calendar based on the differences in tree-ring width. Such a calendar has been made, dating to before 6000 B.C., by collecting examples from many trees and by taking samples from old timbers. This calendar can be compared with samples of old timbers, thus providing a rough idea of the age of ruined buildings (either still standing or buried in the earth). This is most useful in dating buildings made with local timbers, as changes in climate can cause significant differences in tree-ring width.

Compare the tree-ring pattern in tree **B** (left) with that of the piece of timber drawn below left. If this timber were used in a house, when is the earliest date that the house could have been built? You may find it helpful to mark the rings on the edge of a piece of paper and to slide it along the tree trunk until the rings match.

Answers

A question of dates:
1. 38 years old; 2. 44 years; 3. 9 B.C.; 4. A.D. 124.

How old are these trees?
1. 1937; 2. 1882; 3. 1917 and 1934.

How old is this timber?
The most recent tree-ring on the timber matches the one dating to 1921 on tree **B**. A house built using this timber could not therefore have been built before this time.

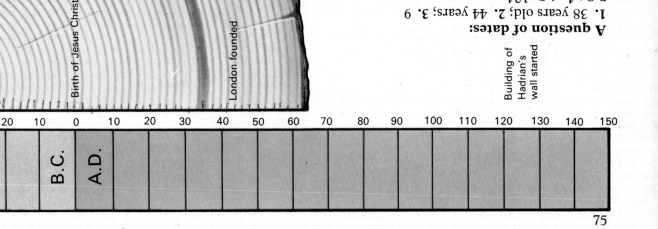

1930

Caesar Augustus became emperor and building of the Pantheon started.

Birth of Jesus Christ

London founded

Building of Hadrian's wall started

| 40 | 30 | 20 | 10 | 0 | 10 | 20 | 30 | 40 | 50 | 60 | 70 | 80 | 90 | 100 | 110 | 120 | 130 | 140 | 150 |

B.C.　A.D.

Glossary

Absolute date: one which can be given in solar years (the time it takes the Earth to revolve around the sun).

Alluvium: the fine mud and rock carried by a fast-moving river and deposited in calm waters or in flooding.

Amphora: an ancient two-handled storage jar, usually wide at the base with a narrow mouth.

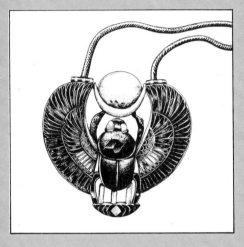

Amulet: a good luck charm.

Archaeology: the study of man-made objects and ruins, usually dating from the ancient past.

Artefact: a man-made object.

Auroch: a now extinct wild ox hunted by prehistoric peoples.

Barrow: a man-made round or elongated mound of earth containing a human burial.

Bier: a platform or litter on which a corpse or coffin is placed.

Canopic jar: a container for the intestines and vital organs of a mummified corpse.

Carbonization: the conversion of objects into charcoal by burning them in an atmosphere which is deficient in oxygen.

Centurion: a Roman non-commissioned officer in charge of a century, originally a hundred legionaries.

Chronology: a system of dating – in the west, a sequence of dates before and after the birth of Jesus Christ.

Concubine: a lawful wife of inferior rank.

Conquistadors: the name given to 16th-century Spanish explorers and conquerors in the Americas.

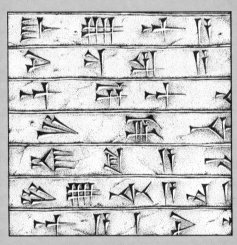

Cuneiform: a Mesopotamian wedge-shaped form of writing, invented by the Sumerians.

Decompression chamber: a cylinder whose air pressure can be raised and lowered; used to help divers with 'the bends'.

Dendrochronology: the tree-ring method of dating ancient objects: a complete sequence of bristlecone pine tree-rings has been established covering at least the last 8100 years; wood cut during this period can be accurately dated by comparison with the sequence.

Determinative: a sign or drawing used by the ancient Egyptians (before vowel signs had been invented) to give a clue to the meaning of words.

Dig: a carefully planned and organized excavation of an archaeological site.

Dynasty: an unbroken line of rulers from the same royal family.

Excavation: the uncovering of an ancient site in a planned and scientific way in order to secure as much information as possible from the site.

Grid: the division of a dig into squares, so that the position of objects discovered in the ruins can be recorded accurately before they are removed. Used on land and underwater sites.

Hieroglyphs: literally, sacred carved letters; the signs of the earliest ancient Egyptian script.

Interpretation: the piecing together of archaeological evidence (such as ruins, broken objects and rubbish) to recreate a picture of the life of the people who once lived on ancient sites; the archaeologist has to use reason and imagination to supply missing information.

Legionary: an ordinary soldier in a Roman legion or army.

Megalith: a huge upright stone.

Millenium: a period of a thousand years.

Mosaic: a work of art, often an ornamental floor in which the picture or design is made of small pieces of coloured stone or glass. called *tessera.*

Mummification: the preservation of a corpse by removing its intestines, treating the body with chemicals and spices and bandaging.

Nomad: literally, a wanderer. A tribe will move from place to place as the seasons change, either in search of ripening plant foods for themselves or as their herds of sheep or cattle search for fresh pasture.

Occupation layer: a layer of ruins or debris representing a definite period of time in the life of a town or village.

Papyrus: a reed growing in Mediterranean lands, particularly Egypt, which was made into bundles to build houses and boats or beaten into a pulp to make an early form of paper.

Patriarch: the all-powerful head or father of a family in the ancient world.

Pharaoh: the title of the rulers of ancient Egypt, who were considered to be both gods and kings and were buried in ornate tombs or pyramids.

Pyramid: a monumental ancient Egyptian tomb in the shape of a tetrahedron containing a pharaoh's burial chamber.

Radio-carbon dating: a method of dating organic materials by establishing the amount of carbon-14 present in them. Firm radio-carbon dates were not possible until a sequence of bristlecone pine tree-rings was established and the carbon-14 content of each ring was measured. It is now possible to give absolute dates for objects whose carbon-14 date can be compared with the bristlecone pine sequence.

Relative date: one which is worked out by the establishment of a sequence of events: an object or event can be dated in this way by comparison with other objects and events, none of which has an absolute date.

Sarcophagus: a coffin or container for a dead body, usually made of stone or terracotta.

Scarab: the sacred dung beetle of the ancient Egyptians, who made models of these insects and used them as amulets.

Site: an area where ancient ruins have been discovered.

Stratum: an occupation layer.

Stratigraphy: the sequence of occupation layers. In theory the oldest layer should be the deepest but archaeologists take into consideration disturbance by later civilizations (for example, digging foundations) and by burrowing animals or natural disturbances.

Tell: a mound resulting from the accumulation of debris from a series of occupation layers on a long-established ancient settlement.

Terracotta: literally, cooked earth. Baked clay used to make a fragile form of pottery.

Tunjo: a South American offering to the gods, usually in the form of a small figure.

Typology: the study of the shape of objects and their arrangement in sequences to show improvements in technique and complexity; sometimes this is used as a kind of relative dating system.

Valhalla: the hall where Viking heroes who died in battle were supposed to spend eternity, alternately feasting and fighting.

Ziggurat: a rectangular temple built in tiers which was originated by the people of ancient Mesopotamia or modern Iraq.

Index
Bold face indicates pages on which illustrations appear.